10/6

157

NO PIOUS PERSON

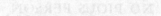

Herbert Hamilton Kelly

HERBERT KELLY, S.S.M.

NO PIOUS PERSON

AUTOBIOGRAPHICAL RECOLLECTIONS

EDITED BY

GEORGE EVERY, S.S.M.

'Talk to me about God and I listen. Talk to me
about your extra superfine saints and I'm not even
interested. I'm mightily interested in small men,
common men, real men; I've always understood
that it was for them in especial that Christ died.'

H.K.

THE FAITH PRESS
7 TUFTON STREET LONDON SW1
MOREHOUSE-BARLOW CO., NEW YORK

PRINTED IN GREAT BRITAIN
in 11pt. Garamond type
BY THE FAITH PRESS LTD.
LEIGHTON BUZZARD

INTRODUCTION

Herbert Hamilton Kelly was born on July 18th, 1860. He was ordained in 1883. The Society of the Sacred Mission was founded by him in 1891; and he remained Director of it, first in Kennington, then in Mildenhall, and finally at Kelham, until 1910. Thereafter he was—what? For a few years he taught theology in Japan. He was a familiar figure until into the 'thirties at the summer conferences of the Student Christian Movement—an eccentric character, unquestionably of importance, somewhat elliptically related to the concerns of other Christians. When the Second World War came, he was a very old man, shuffling about the corridors at Kelham and at the end confined to his room, impatient and anxious to be gone. He died on October 31st, 1950.

It does not immediately appear from this outline of Fr. Kelly's life and work [1] that there is any reason for the general public to bother with 'the old man' (as he was called during the second half of his life). If you are interested in the development of the religious life in the technical sense ('monks and nuns') in the Church of England—yes. If you have an interest in the by-ways of theological history—perhaps. But if you have not lived your Christian life within the Anglo-Catholic tradition what is the importance for you of Fr. Kelly and Kelham? These questions require answers and it is the purpose of this introduction to suggest the answers at which I have arrived in the attempt, with the aid of friends, to answer them for myself. They are, in brief: that Kelly contributed far more than has been generally realized to the development of the Ecumenical Movement; that his astonishing success in Japan has important implications for missionaries; that he made an important contribution to theological education, and that his approach to philosophy and theology is of a kind which makes it important and interesting to intelligent 'secular' people to-day and not merely to the authorities of theological colleges; and, above all, that he is abundantly worth knowing, as he can be

---

[1] There is an admirable memoir of Fr. Kelly by Brother George Every, S.S.M., prefixed to the 1959 reissue of *The Gospel of God* (S.C.M. Press).

known through his own autobiographical writings, for the quality of his 'impiety' as of his piety.

• • •

The drawing together of Christians in a common search for the unity of the Church, as Christ wills it, is an outstanding feature of this century. Much of it is, and must remain, hidden, as Christians seek to enter together into the eternal prayer of their Lord. Much of it has assumed an outward and public form in the successive movements of practical co-operation, common theological discussion, and negotiations towards corporate reunion. The Ecumenical Movement properly understood includes both the movement of prayer for unity which was given so profound an impetus by Abbé Paul Couturier [2] and also what is sometimes called the 'organized Ecumenical Movement' associated with the World Council of Churches,[3] and there is an increasing depth of mutual understanding and affection between the leaders of the two 'wings.'

The movements which, beginning in the later decades of the nineteenth century, have come together since the last war in the World Council of Churches, started in the Protestant missionary world, and their main financial and numerical strength is still in the Churches of the Reformation. But the Ecumenical Movement, once it came to self-understanding—the symbolic date is 1910, the year of the first World Missionary Conference at Edinburgh— has never been content to be 'Pan-Protestant.' It has sought to reach out into the Anglo-Catholic, the Eastern Orthodox, and the Roman Catholic worlds, for the Lord prayed that they *all* might be one. As early as the years when 'Edinburgh 1910' was being prepared, the ecumenical task was seen in these inclusive terms, and this was because the problem had already been faced in the British Student Christian Movement and a solution found in what was called the 'interdenominational position.' That the British S.C.M. had developed this position at all is largely due to the influence within it of Herbert Kelly and Neville Talbot.

The Edinburgh Conference was overwhelmingly an assembly of missionaries in the various traditions of Evangelical Protestantism.

[2] See *The Abbé Paul Couturier: Apostle of Christian Unity* by A. M. Allchin (Faith Press, 1960).
[3] See *The History of the Ecumenical Movement 1517–1948* edited by Ruth Rouse and Stephen Charles Neill (London, S.P.C.K., 1954).

There were of course no Orthodox; the Society for the Propagation of the Gospel had declined to be formally represented. But a number of S.P.G. leaders were present unofficially; and the Archbishop of Canterbury gave an address. Organizing the stewards was Neville Talbot, the son of E. S. Talbot, then Bishop of Southwark and a leading High Churchman, one of an enormous clan of Talbots, Lyttletons and others of great influence in the Church of England. In the wings, backstage as usual, was Fr. Kelly: some of his comments on the Conference will be found on pp. 110–18 of this book. E. S. Talbot explained his own presence and that of other Anglican High Churchmen (such as Bishop Charles Gore) across the lunch-table to a group of Scottish divines: 'We would not have been here in this Conference had it not been for the S.C.M.'

The traditional basis of co-operation among Evangelical Protestants had been to put on one side those matters which divided (such as differing beliefs about infant baptism or the episcopate) and work together on the basis of those things that were held in common. If every one is 'low church' this is a sensible and honest basis: and in the ecclesiastical atmosphere of the time it was almost certainly the only possible way to start. But once people turn up to whom 'denominational differences' are *not* unimportant or peripheral and for whom an 'undenominational' Christianity leaves out things by which they live, the *un*denominational solution will serve no longer. This problem presented itself early in the history of the British S.C.M. with the presence in it of Catholic Anglicans such as Kelly and Talbot, and their presence led the S.C.M. to work out its *inter*denominational position, which assumes that each must bring the fullness of his convictions and which works for a unity in which our deep differences are not ignored but transcended. A situation was created where Baptists and Presbyterians and Anglicans and Orthodox could work together in religious (and not merely social) work without compromising their convictions and where the remaining separations (which are often focussed in the Catholic refusal of intercommunion) may and do cause pain to all but do not destroy—they may even help to deepen —the fellowship.

This has led to a steady move away from the kind of approach to reunion which is at bottom concerned with adjusting inherited convictions, to the recognition that we look for a unity which transcends our differences. The perception, therefore, of Abbé Couturier that we can all and must all pray for the unity which Christ wills when He wills it, leads to the conviction that unions between Churches less deeply divided than the Church of Rome is from the Protestant Churches, must be potentially more inclusive. A new scheme of union must not make a wider reunion more difficult but, by releasing spiritual energies from ancient shackles, foster a yet further recovery of the fullness of Christ.[4]

Much of this understanding of ecumenism has been painfully won in the decades since 1910, but an essential foundation was laid then in the early years of the British S.C.M. Neville Talbot gave the S.C.M. what may be crudely termed some entré into ecclesiastical high society; Kelly gave it a stream of young men at its conferences in such sort that the Catholic tradition was always present to the Protestant majority in the Movements, and in a form which was friendly and open; and he gave it the stimulus of himself.

Other men and other movements were involved; and one should not try to claim too much for Fr. Kelly. But I do not think my Presbyterian father was wrong in picking out Kelly's contribution as crucial:

'Such men as Father Kelly of the S.S.M. did two things for crowds of the members of the Student Movement whom he met at the summer camps. One was that he incarnated a life of Christian devotion to which the obedience, fellowship and cultus of the Church were essential. The second was that in mastering this fact they found also that the Church was divided, deeply divided, and that the earnest camaraderie of their own evangelistic and missionary fellowship had no automatic remedy for this state of division.'[5]

From that day to this, there has never been lacking a group of

---

[4] Cf. Fr. Henry St. John, O.P., in the introduction to *Approaches to Christian Unity* by C. J. Dumont, O.P. (London: Darton, Longman and Todd, 1960): 'But there is also a considerable and increasing element in the Ecumenical Movement, especially in the Faith and Order section of it, which recognizes that the only unity which is in accordance with Christ's will is unity which has belief as its basis. This element tends to insist that it is impossible to leave the Church of Rome out of account in any fruitful work for the unity of Christians' (p. 9).

[5] William Paton in *Theology*, October, 1939, pp. 259–60.

Kelham students at S.C.M. Summer Conferences. Fr. Kelly has indicated what this connection meant to the Society of the Sacred Mission in its early struggles for recognition, and I sense that it means something still. Certainly Kelham is, as it always has been, both a religious community unequivocally within the Catholic tradition and at the same time extraordinarily open and welcoming and grateful to people who are not, and feel no call to become, monks or catholics. What all this has meant not only to the S.C.M. but to the Christian world generally is incalculable.

However, it should not be supposed that 'the old man' took the S.C.M. at its own valuation, or approved of its successive enthusiasms. Had Fr. Kelly been a more typical High Churchman, he might have been profoundly suspicious of the trends of thought expounded in the main meetings of summer conferences. In the early 'thirties he defined the current party-line as 'God is nice and in Him is no nastiness at all,' and his general reaction to S.C.M. Swanwick conferences is summed up in the dictum: 'The main meetings are awful; but the ragging is divine.' This is perhaps as elliptical as his famous remark that the pigs at Kelham were the prime proof of the Resurrection. He liked the ragging and the practical joking (which was a feature of those days much diminished in these) because he thought it proper to a large gathering of young people and showed that they were alive and open— and perhaps also because it was congenial to his own temperament. At all events, there exists a photograph, dating from about 1910, of Fr. Kelly in his habit sitting triumphant on the greasy pole with a defeated opponent (said by oral tradition at Kelham to be William Temple) feet upwards on the ground beneath him. There is faintly discernible on Fr. Kelly's face a smirk of satisfaction. He liked all this. Had he been one to hold his views with defensive rigidity or tremble for the Ark of God, he would have been worried by the doctrine expounded in the main meetings; being Kelly, he was unimpressed, and took them with no great seriousness. Anyway, he never attached overmuch importance to the opinions of men, being preoccupied with the fact of God.

But, approving or disapproving, he was there, a Catholic religious in a more or less liberal Protestant gathering, welcome, somewhat puzzling, saying things that would fall into perspective

9

and be better understood only when, after he himself had ceased to go to conferences, the British began to pay attention to Karl Barth and the Anglicans among them had begun to rediscover F. D. Maurice (whom Kelly had never forgotten); and he was in himself a forcible reminder that Catholicism was something with which it was necessary and might even be possible to come to terms.

When one considers how easy it is for Catholics to flinch from Protestants into an 'ecumenism' that confines itself to Rome and the Orthodox, and for Protestants to elaborate a sort of 'ecumenism' which Catholics can share only by shedding so much that is integral to their experience of God in Christ, it is difficult to overestimate the significance of what Kelly meant for us all; and the ecumenical section of the writings in this book are an important source for the church history of our time.

Kelly's own view is summed up in *Catholicity* [6] : 'I think that what S. Paul said of human religions is equally true of our schisms : 'The times of this ignorance God winked at, but now commands all men everywhere to repent.' . . . I do not think men are ever wholly wrong, except in thinking they are wholly right.' It is not surprising that Dr. W. A. Visser 't Hooft, now General Secretary of the World Council of Churches, should have written in 1933 that Fr. Kelly 'comes perhaps nearer to combining in his life and teaching all that is best in Catholicism and in Protestantism than any other Christian alive.' [7]

. . .

Secondly, one who has been a missionary senses that there is, for any one concerned with the planting and development of the Christian Church in Africa and Asia, and with the relation of the newer Churches of those lands with the older Churches of the West, something extremely important locked up in the story of Fr. Kelly's stay in Japan between 1913 and 1919. In that time he made an impression on the Nippon Sei Ko Kai (the Anglican Church in Japan) which is generally reckoned to be unique; and his influence is strong and powerful to this day.

[6] London, 1932.
[7] W. A. Visser 't Hooft, *Anglo-Catholicism and Orthodoxy: A Protestant View* (London, 1933).

Before he went to Japan he had already worked out a theory about the role of the missionary. In *The Church and Religious Unity* [8] he had written: 'The missionaries . . . ensure that the Indian or Chinese Church shall not drift away from the fundamental basis. But after the first beginning has been made the work of expansion lies with the Church itself. We do not want the heathen without to become English Christians, but Indian Christians, Chinese or African Christians, as the case may be. . . . The true work of evangelization, the making of converts, should be carried on by the Christians living there, and not by the missionaries. Only an Indian can really preach Indian Christianity to Indians. . . . The Christians will understand even an English missionary, for Christianity is a bond between them, but the English missionary preaching to heathens is not in his right place.' This point of view he applied to England: 'Ministers of any denomination are a people apart. The religion of a man to whom religion is the main business of life, and the religion of a man who uses it to consecrate other business are bound to be different. . . . The priest is the priest, and the minister is the minister, of God's Church. The lay Christian is the priest of God's universe, and it is mainly his business to preach to them that are without.'

This point of view went with him to Japan. There, as his manner was, Kelly asked questions of a disconcerting kind, and talked about God in his indirect and puzzling way. Brother George Every suggests that his success in Japan was due to the likeness in Japanese eyes of this consecrated monk with his hard questions to the traditional sage of Zen Buddhism. He was certainly detached from the usual course of the missionary career: he never learned Japanese, and was clearly not a 'regular missionary'; but he was equally distinct—and not only by his habit—from a more ordinary academic scholar such as might give a few years to helping to start a theological college, which is what Fr. Kelly was doing. He was also in the content of his doctrine distinguishable from the other Anglicans, let alone from the American Protestants with what he called their 'Modernisms.' This is all described in his own words in Chapter IX of this book.

Hidden in these six years are almost certainly things that the

[8] London, 1913. The quotations are from pp. 194–5.

whole Church needs to know, and they will be found, I think, in the way in which he worked out his convictions in practice. We need to know *what* he said and did and *how* he said and did them. His own account of Kelham is called 'An Idea in the Working'— I for one want to know what is to be learned from Fr. Kelly's 'idea of a missionary in the working.' This is something that only his Japanese friends can tell us, but perhaps they need our questions to get at the answers: and this is a study which ought to be undertaken soon, before the opportunity is lost for ever.

It might be of value to the Church in Japan as well as to ourselves. Few men have made in what is relatively so short a time so great an impact on an alien Church. But there are signs that in Japan, as in Britain, 'the old man' might have been disconcerted by some of the developments to which his pupils gave their enthusiasms (not that his judgment would necessarily be final or infallible). A recent visitor to Japan felt that loyalty to the Kelly tradition had in some cases come to mean having the right Catholic worship and the right Catholic teaching and waiting with these blessings for people to come and be converted. Perhaps in Japan, as in Britain, there is a time-lag before Fr. Kelly can come into his own.

• • •

A third significance of Fr. Kelly lies in his understanding of education, of theological education, and of the meaning of theology itself. His principal educational point was that students must be taught to learn and to think for themselves. This is apparently an elementary point; but when one thinks of the number and popularity of little books with which theological students may cram themselves with potted facts and approved opinions not only against examinations but also and much more dangerously against a future of delivering sermons and preparing people for confirmation and so on, perhaps it is not so obvious after all. Kelly held that the weaker students are intellectually, the more important it is that they should think for themselves about real questions raised in their own minds, and not about objections put up by an apologetic theologian to be knocked down again. So one could almost say that he devoted his life to asking unexpected questions, to rubbing people's noses in ordinary common un-idealistic objects such as pigs and frogs' legs (rather than sunsets and majestic mountains), in the effort to get them to take the universe seriously. From this came his passionate interest in science—though characteristically he called it dabbling—'Since I began to think, I have dabbled in a whole host of things—science, philosophy, psychology, history, Biblical criticism, to say nothing of law, economics, and many more. . . . I boggled at Darwinism a long time, though the monkeys never troubled me (Mendelism when I heard of it, was a great joy).' [9]

The course at Kelham therefore demands a philosophical preparation before theology proper is tackled. This preparation includes psychology, ancient and modern logic, a bit of Plato, Locke, Hume, and some attention to biology and genetics. Only then is any theological subject treated dogmatically.

This is the centre of the Kelham course, and the meaning of 'dogmatics' that Kelly gave to Kelham. 'Dogmatics' is a tricky word in English—it suggests a suave parson handing out packaged 'dogma'—and this (it need hardly be said) was not what Kelly aimed at. The nature of Kelham dogmatics can be illustrated by two contrasts.

Neither Kelly nor Kelham has produced, or is likely to produce, a massive dogmatic system on the German model. Kelly was far from insensitive to the German theologians, and the friend of mine who read *The Gospel of God* for the first time the other day and said, 'Great heavens! This is pure Bonhoeffer,' [10] was not far off the mark. He would have appreciated Karl Heim's attempt to grapple with the meaning of modern science, and I think he would have sympathized with Bonhoeffer's plea for a 'religion-less Christianity,' for a life of Christians with God in Christ that is not dependent on the whole framework of 'religion' and can exist and flourish in a world where men have outgrown religion as superstition and think that they have outgrown God too. But what of Karl Barth—not the Barth of *From Rousseau to Ritschl*

[9] *The Gospel of God,* p. 43.
[10] Dietrich Bonhoeffer was a young German theologian and ecumenical leader who was martyred by the Nazis in the closing days of the war. His books, especially *The Cost of Discipleship* and *Letters and Papers from Prison* (S.C.M. Press), are widely read in Britain. The latter is also available in the Fontana series (Collins).

with its sympathetic approach to many makers of the modern mind, but the Barth of those imposing volumes of *Church Dogmatics?* If he had come in the end to agree with the common British view (which may be a misunderstanding) that this kind of theology refuses to have any commerce with philosophy or science, being based purely upon the Word of God, he would have reacted violently against it in the name of reason and of science. If it is true that theology is running away from experimental science, and running faster every decade, Kelly's refusal to put 'biblical theology' at the centre of the theological course may be seen to have been justified. For him it was indeed vitally important, but it was not the centre—it was essential material to be worked into our own theological thinking when, after a course of having our noses rubbed in the universe, we are ready for it.

The difference between Kelly's view of theological education and another Anglican ideal may be sharply illustrated by a personal reminiscence. When I was Chaplain at Westcott House, Cambridge, in 1946 I went to stay for a few days at Kelham. B. K. Cunningham, 'the best loved man in the Church of England' (whose *Life* was admirably written by Dr. J. R. H. Moorman, now Bishop of Ripon), had, as Principal successively of Bishop's Hostel, Farnham, and of Westcott House, Cambridge, exercised an enormous influence on the Church of England. Fr. Kelly, hearing that I was at Kelham, sent for me. It was the last time I saw him, and as he sat in bed, wrapped in an old shawl, looking at once formidable and rather scruffy, I talked as best I could through an ear-trumpet which appeared to have been constructed from parts of an old bicycle pump.

'So you're at Westcott House,' he said.

'Yes, Father.'

'I envy B.K.'

'Why, Father?'

'He's dead.'

There was a pause. I waited to see what he would say next.

'I can't forgive B.K. for turning out all those young men who haven't got a gospel.'

This is not the place (nor have I the equipment) to attempt a discriminating summing-up of that debate. But one may observe that Kelly had put his finger on something which is characteristic of one sort of Anglican theological college. The sons of B.K., deeply as they would resent the aspersion on 'The Professor,' would not attempt to argue that a sustained attention to theology is the special quality of Westcott House. Another College Principal has observed in private conversation that there seems to him in the tradition of his college to be a gap between the critical study of the New Testament undertaken in the most radically scientific way and the steady discipline of worship and prayer in the Catholic tradition. This gap cannot be filled by 'biblical theology' *tout court*, valuable as its aid can be, for it does not meet the philosophical issues involved in historical criticism; but it can be filled by dogmatics as Kelly understood it.

And yet, oddly enough, 'the Professor' and 'the old man' were closer than they knew. B. K. Cunningham had a limited enthusiasm for theology partly no doubt because that is in the English tradition, but also and more deeply because he feared that by it men might be drilled into an orthodoxy and be hindered by a party-line from becoming what God meant them to be. Fr. Kelly desired that men should *think* truly about God and His world and His ways with it; but he thought that often much labour was required to get them to do so. Neither of them had any use for reach-me-down orthodoxies; and both of them believed much more in God than in religion.

This is the distinction with which *The Gospel of God* begins: 'I am trying to write a book about God, and the place God has in our life. In the common way of talking what is concerned with God is called religion. . . . I want to insist that God and Religion are not quite the same. . . .' This of course echoes F. D. Maurice: 'God is not the same as religion; the church and sacraments are also realities, far greater than our theories about them; and the theories, even negative theories, are witnessing to positive realities.' In the decades when Maurice was little read and before the revival of theology in our own day, this was an unusual way of putting things.[11] For us, it can be life-giving.

[11] In the years when Kelly himself was not understood, much of his teaching (as that of his master, F. D. Maurice) found expression in the widely influential work of one of the most distinguished members of his community, Fr. Gabriel Hebert, S.S.M.

I have tried to show that Kelly is important for the contemporary discussion about the nature of theological education. But his importance is a good bit wider than that, and is connected with the widespread conviction on the part of laymen that very few theologians seem to address themselves to any one but other theologians. During this century it has become harder and harder for theologians to make themselves understood by the intelligent non-Christian or the Christian layman who is trying to think Christianly while truly involved in the 'secular' world where God has called him. In part, this is due to forces within philosophy and biology and physics; in part it is due to a proneness on the part of theologians to retreat into a private world of biblical theology, church history, and ecclesiastical concerns, whither secular people neither can nor wish to accompany them. There are not many theologians able and willing to talk candidly about the known and the physical —the world around us—as they see it in the light of God. Kelly does this, for his own preoccupations with the common things and stubborn facts, with how people's minds work and what interests them, can find an echo amongst intellectuals concerned with the evidential significance of the senses, and the world at large obsessed with 'doing it yourself.'

. . .

An attempt must be made finally to say something about Fr. Kelly's austerity. There is a tough, implacable side to his teaching and his life, which is none-the-less entirely compatible with the jokes and the love of pigs. It comes out starkly enough in the *Principles* of the Society of the Sacred Mission. Here for example is what he wrote *Concerning choice of Work*:

> You may not choose your work; indeed, count not yourself worthy of any work.
> You may prefer, however, that which is most dangerous, least notable, least popular. There will generally be room for you here.
> Seek that which is lowest and most servile. This you can nearly always do safely.
> Many read of washing the disciples' feet, who think themselves above cleaning another man's boots.
> It is better to serve the least esteemed than the great. The service of the king is a high honour for which nobles contend, but to be the servant of the poor and contemptible is to imitate Christ.

If, however, you should be called to high and spiritual work, you may indeed fear and tremble, but you are not permitted to refuse as though you doubted your own powers, for you ought to be quite sure of your own incapacity—and of God's strength.

These are matters on which Fr. Kelly's sons, the fathers and brethren of his Society, have the best, perhaps the only, title to be heard. The Society however is, as it has always been, very open to other people. Indeed, it must sometimes feel that it takes considerable risks, with a hundred theological students and up to fifteen visitors at a time living in the mother-house with the main body of the professed, and not in a separate college or guesthouse. If so, its friends must be grateful for the extent to which they can share its life and the heritage of Fr. Kelly. But the deepest understanding must necessarily, and rightly, be reserved for those who have been called to serve God in the fellowship of the Rule of the Society.

Even so, a glimpse may be afforded. I was present, as it happens, at the last engagement outside Kelham, a retreat that he conducted for members of the staff of the Student Christian Movement in 1938. It took place in a retreat house full of religious bric-à-brac of an old-fashioned Anglo-Catholic type, which must have been as distasteful to him as to his audience. For most of us it was our first retreat, and for many of us, the whole idea of a retreat was strange—I remember that there were debates about how far we should be compelled to be silent, but I remember little else. But one thing has lived with me ever since, a sentence-ending from one of the addresses, '. . . and then you might miss being crucified; and that would be a pity.'

I have tried to live with that, and by it. In the end, that is really why I try to go to Kelham whenever I can, to slip into the life of the place, to be stimulated by the thoughts of friends in the Society, to say my prayers in that terrific Chapel which is one of his monuments, and to seek the will of God for me and to see myself more clearly, with the aid of the tough quizzical integrity of Fr. Kelly.

DAVID M. PATON

B

I

Mainly from notes left by Father Kelly
and his brother, Father Alfred

[Fr. Kelly's great-grandfather was an Irish labourer from Belfast who came to Glasgow with the first wave of immigration at the beginning of the nineteenth century. He was a Protestant, and probably married a Scotswoman, since his son, James, was described by his grandson as 'a typical Manchester Scot,' who made money ('I never knew how'), but never spent it. 'He lived and died cottage-wise. I never remember a servant.' He lived until 1889, so all his grandchildren must have known him.

The family's considerable properties came partly from him, and partly through the marriage of his son with Margaret Alice Eccles, one of the two daughters and heiresses of Joseph Eccles, a landowner and mill-owner at Mill Hill, just outside Blackburn. Joseph Eccles built a Congregational chapel, and married into a Wesleyan family, but some members of his family must have conformed to the Church of England before his daughter married an Anglican clergyman in 1856, for a collection of sermons and pamphlets made by Fr. Kelly's father includes a funeral sermon for William Eccles, preached at S. John's Church, Blackburn.[1]

James Davenport Kelly, the son of James, and father of our Fr. Kelly, was born in 1829. He distinguished himself at Manchester Grammar School, where he was the first Lawson medalist in 1847, and won a scholarship at Wadham College, Oxford, where he took a second class honours degree in *literae humaniores,* and won the Hody Hebrew exhibition and the Kennicott Hebrew scholarship. He seems to have had academic ambitions, for he was ordained deacon in the diocese of Oxford, but he did not secure a fellowship, and became a curate at Blackburn before he was ordained priest. From 1856–60 he was Vice-Principal of S. Elizabeth's College, Guernsey. It was then that he married, and his first children were born.

His children were under the impression that he did a good deal of reading in the early part of his life, but that his intellectual interests, whatever they were, had ceased to develop before they were old enough for serious conversation. In later life however he gave some lectures, chiefly on the Psalms, in the Bishop's School at Manchester, which

---

[1] By the incumbent, the Revd. H. J. Marlen, on Sunday, June 26th, 1853.

prepared men for holy orders by a two years' course of home study. He was also vice-principal, and did much to support the school. 'He definitely preferred the day school to the boarding school,' and Fr. Alfred thought that he preferred curates 'from the ranks' to university men. He was not in any sense a theologian.

He had become essentially a man of action. He returned to Manchester in 1860, as Rector of S. James's, George Street, moving in 1865 to Christ Church, Ashton-under-Lyne, where he remained for more than eighteen years. In 1884 he became a canon of Manchester Cathedral and Rector of S. Matthew's, Manchester. At about this time he was offered, and refused, the see of Barbados in the West Indies. He later seems to have regretted this refusal, but his children thought that he would not have been happy out of his own country, and that even on English holidays he missed Manchester.

He was a steady Evangelical in his churchmanship, but avoided controversy. When his children developed other views, he made little or no attempt to stop this, and defended them staunchly against criticism from his fellow-clergy. His leading characteristics were 'devotion to duty and family affection.' 'He worked assiduously and went on working till a few days before he died. But he never overdid it, e.g. he never sat up late, and he never worried. Like Wellington and Napoleon he could always sleep, both at night, and by snatches in the day.' He did little or nothing to form directly the minds of his family. 'He couldn't do that without giving them opportunities for discussion, and discussion as much as controversy was not in his line.' But his indirect influence was considerable, and perhaps greater than they allowed.[2]

'He made a point of holding himself straight ("upright as a pine," said *The Church Times*) when he was eighty. He hated being ill, and it was an insult to suggest, or to notice, that he had a cold. He was speaking in the open air quite a short time before he died, and walking in procession too, during an all-Manchester mission.' He and his wife died close together in April and May, 1912, when he was eighty-three

[2] His one printed sermon, on self-sacrifice, preached on his departure from Blackburn in December, 1855, does contain some passages which might have been his son's:

'The study of science, the reading of a lecture, the care of bodily health, conversation with friends, are no longer to be looked upon as trifles, or purely personal considerations. They are all parts of a whole, and therefore, each in its place, to be improved to the utmost extent, that we may be more fit for our lifelong calling.

'Even in our more direct efforts for the improvement of our own and our brethren's souls we are often put to shame by the energy, the restless activity, the multifarious diligence of the world around us. Verily "the children of this world are in their generation wiser than the children of light." '

and she seventy-six. We have no such detailed picture of her, but 'saint' is the word her children naturally used of her, and clearly she engaged their confidence far more than their father. Fr. Kelly's letters to her cover all his hopes, fears, and interests. One, which will be quoted hereafter, gives his reactions to the World Missionary Conference at Edinburgh little more than a year before her death.

Of the other children, the eldest brother, Arthur, joined the army and rose to be a Brigadier. The second, Francis, was like his father a Lawson medallist at Manchester Grammar School. He won a scholarship to Trinity College, Cambridge, but was taken ill and died before he was twenty-three, in 1882. He had great influence at the Grammar School and at home, and was clearly a very powerful factor in Herbert's life ('my chum brother'), but we know very little about him. Edith Mary, the 'chum sister,' born in 1862, remained at home until her parents died, but very shortly afterwards joined the Community of the Epiphany at Truro. She worked in Japan from 1919–28, just after Father Kelly's return from that country, and died in 1931.

Of the younger children one became a doctor, and died in 1910; another sister married. The youngest brother, Alfred Davenport Kelly, born in 1872, played no part in Fr. Kelly's family background, since he was a baby when he went to Manchester Grammar School, and no more than a boy of eleven when he was ordained, but he played a large part in his life, since he followed him to London to be a curate at S. John's, Kennington, in the very early days of his foundation, and made his profession in the Society of the Sacred Mission at Mildenhall in 1900. He was the Society's first provincial superior in South Africa, where he worked for many years before returning to Kelham as a tutor in Old Testament, logic, and literature. Like his brother he was a keen mountaineer, but unlike him he was also a brilliant athlete, who played tennis with great skill and verve until near the end of his life. He died in March 1950 at the age of seventy-seven.]

What is cleverness? I take it that people generally mean a natural facility or quickness in picking up a right way of doing things without needing to be told how they should be done, or having to find out a method by conscious reflection, or laboured practice. Both reflection and practice are necessary to any high degree of perfection, but in the really clever the reflection is mostly unconscious, and the practice is a natural joy in fulfilment. Neither is a basis of attainment.

Every one of us possesses some degree of this natural facility.

Most people possess a good deal. It is the basis of all common-sense action in ordinary social relations, and in ordinary trade. The French phrase *'savoir faire'* is better than the English. In all the ordinary and simple affairs of life, we have perfected ourselves by an enormous amount of practice. It is only in rarer things —certain sciences, and in difficult sports—that exceptional cleverness shows itself. Everybody can do simple arithmetic; not every one can do higher mathematics. I suppose none of us has any idea of the subtlety and skill with which we handle a fork (try chopsticks), yet the larger number of those who play tennis seem to be incapable of grasping even what they are supposed to do with a racket, while others get the idea almost at once.

I stress the distinction between the conscious and unconscious. Most naturally clever people have hardly any idea how they do things, still less of the scientific reasons why this way is right. Without talking about forks, few first-class cricketers know how they make their strokes, or how they know at once which to use. They can show you, and the coach has a number of set rules, which he imparts as required, though he quite often omits the points most primary and vital to a beginner, because to the coach they were so obvious that they never wanted learning at all. Only here and there a consummate player, like C. B. Fry, explains the science with mathematical diagrams.

Cleverness is, of course, somewhat rare. Indeed, as it seems to me, we only call a man clever because his cleverness is exceptional, i.e. above what most of us possess. It is a curious thing that it is, nevertheless, the only thing most people understand. I distinguished above between 'rules' as to how a thing should be done, like the 'follow through' of a stroke, and the scientific reason why it is right. In the result, the ordinary player believes success will come by practice (even though he is practising the wrong things). He may listen to a rule, but scientific explanations take no hold on his mind at all; probably that is why he can make so little use of the rules given him. Quite often he is impatient of both. 'Shall I show you *how* to use your bat?' said W. G. (Grace) to a Blackheath guttersnipe. 'Wot does an old buffer like you know about cricket?' was the indignant answer.

Nothing is so natural as mannerism, or so artificial as the

apparently natural. Reminiscences of childhood are futile and often silly, but I go back to them to find what was really natural or innate, as distinguished from the effect of circumstances or of acquired character. So far as I know myself, and remember from the very beginning, I was, continued, and remain exceptionally stupid, i.e. incapable of picking up the obvious thing to do, even in regard to customary manners. One of my earliest reminiscences is the constant and amazed reply of elders, and not less of brothers and sisters, to the questions: 'Can I do this?' or 'What should I do?'—'Of course not' or 'Of course,' and—the pathetic protest of stupidity—'Why is everything "of course"?' Why am I supposed to know what I have never been told? Why indeed? Except that they all did know, and most people do, but I never did.

I started Latin when I was seven or eight. I learnt cases, and rules for their use; then I wrote exercises. At about ten I started Cæsar. I remember now my utter amazement at how any one was supposed to know how to disentangle the sentences. I never solved that mystery till at thirty I wanted to read S. Thomas, and discovered for myself that, if you began with the main verb, and then picked out its subject and object, everything would fall into place.

I did rather better with mathematics, where there were demonstrable rules for everything, but of all I learnt at school, only physics (heat) and physiology stuck by me. They were bye studies in the classical forms, but here was something that not only had rules on which the results followed, but had explanations as to why it was so. Preparing for Woolwich I also tried my hand at chemistry. I was set to laboratory analysis, and I carried out set blow-pipe experiments, but here I had no conception what I was supposed to be doing. I was also baffled by lack of memory, for, in chemistry, there is a good deal to remember. We used—like most schoolboys—to learn repetition, especially Latin. We used to have questions in the terminal exams. I never attempted them. It never occurred to me that you could be seriously expected to remember a few hundred lines learnt weeks before. To remember them till the next morning was as much as I could hope.

The naturally clever pick up their rules or ways of doing things often without formulating them at all. Even 'Cavendish,' the great exponent of the science of whist, being asked why he played a certain card, could only answer: 'Because I should have been a fool if I hadn't.' But beyond instinct for the right thing, there is a cleverness, or facility, in recognizing rules. (Thus 'Cavendish' wrote his books.) I had no cleverness at all. I did mathematics up to differential calculus well enough to get into Woolwich, and afterwards to get a third in Honour Moderations at Oxford. I was taught exactly thus far by a very good tutor, and I never got any further. I followed his *viva voce* explanations quite well, but I do not conceive that they were at all different from those given in the books, which I could not follow. I cannot make out why it should have been so.

As a result, I was always looking for general rules, and that brought me to a certain sympathy with what I called 'the scientific aspect.' I was glad to get at the principles or reasons on which the rule rested. It gave the rule a certain solidity, and, since you could fall back on the reason to recover the rule, it took the weight off the feeble string of my memory. I remember saying once that I remembered the Lord's Prayer best by recalling the sequence of its ideas. I remember a passage in a book I read as a boy, about people 'who drink tea by strategy, and tell the clock by algebra.' I was chuckling over it at Oxford, recognizing a fairly correct description of how my mind worked.

I took refuge in ideas—i.e. in rules, and, if I could get them, in the reasons for rules, but it was years before I acquired any facility in learning these things; it was years before I learnt to find them for myself. I had a friend at Woolwich who was really clever at mathematics, and also at chemistry. He could play with them joyously. I stared, wonderingly, dumbly, at what he was doing, and how he did it. One thing I did learn, and I learnt it from my helplessness. I never scoffed. I never had the least tendency or temptation to be impatient about ideas, methods, reasons for things. There are a good few folk to whom I should like to say: 'If you had ever been as big a fool as I was, you would not take the foolish attitude you do now.'

From this natural incapacity, it followed that I was a very unsocial and lonely soul. I was at a boarding school for some two years, but I stood quite outside the life of the other boys. They played games. I wandered about outside. I did not know what they were doing. At that time I did not know what I was doing either. I was not exactly miserable. I had no idea what happiness was; consequently I was not in general unhappy. Sometimes I was. My one instinct was to hide it in a sort of impassive reticence. At this boarding-school we used to parade for church in top hats. My hat was—or the school said it was—of a wrong shape. I was very sensitive and I suffered horribly. Nothing would have been easier than to get a new one at home. I was not too proud to give way; it never so much as occurred to me to do it—in that or any other matter. If you had to suffer, you had to, and must wait till it was over. I remember saying to myself, 'it can't go on for ever,' when the family was letting me have it over a bad school report.

I understand the psychologists say that the inferiority-complex makes a man assertive. I daresay it does with forcible people. I had no forcibleness, no strength of will, in me. I hardly know if I was conscious of inferiority, though I had reason to be. Whatever it was, I armoured myself in that same reticent impassivity. It was enough if I could keep out of people's way.

I might have grown out of these defects, but circumstances were all the other way. Father was an extraordinarily forcible and capable man. I think that habit of reticence came from him. Mother was a devoted saint, but both were very unsocial. We lived from 1865 to 1884 outside a second-rate manufacturing town. What little 'society' there was lived on the opposite side. Visitors were very rare; entertaining, totally unknown either there or afterwards in Manchester.

During my boyhood, from eleven to seventeen, I attended the Manchester Grammar School. After an early breakfast, we went in six miles by train, and came back directly school was over. I knew one boy from Ashton of whom I saw a good deal. I knew no others. I do remember a few entertainments which I enjoyed greatly. Possibly if I had had more, I might have been different. Some of my younger brothers and sisters, when we were in Manchester, became sociable, but there was this difference. Father and Mother did not care for society; I was afraid of it. I did not know what people were doing or would expect me to do.

I lived very much in a world of my own. I had a chum brother,

25

extraordinarily able. He went home (*sc.* died) while I was an undergraduate. I had a chum sister. At about sixteen I decided on the army and began to prepare for Woolwich. My eldest brother had gone there before. Then two things happened. The first was my conversion. If I tell that story, I will tell it somewhere else. I will only say that my religious conceptions were of the narrowest, evangelical and pietistic kind. I had never conceived of any other. Secondly, about that time, I began to be deaf.

I duly passed into Woolwich. It was a bit of a nightmare. The cadets were nearly all public school boys, well used to a common life, of indifferent morals and no religion. I was desperately shy—which, of course, they did not understand. Religion was less than no help to me; I mean, it did not help me to understand them, and, needless to say, they did not understand me. I believe now that many of them were really good Christians. I could play no games, and dared not try. I might have pulled through if it had not been for deafness—I like to think that I might—but that was fatal. There were a few bad breaks from not hearing orders, but the real difficulty was that it threw me back on my passion for reticence. I kept out of people's way in order to hide the defect, when the one necessity was to mix, and to make the best of people. It was the 'top hat' over again. If the men had been nice, I might have learnt something, but I was to them an exasperatingly odd fish—'too big a fool' they would have said. I do not demur, though I think 'too stupid' is more accurate.

Yet I would not have missed it, nor the misery of it, for the world. Is there anything in life so morally disastrous as the claim to happiness? I read it afterwards in Carlyle—'O vain mortal, what is there in the constitution of things why thou shouldst be happy?' What difference does it make? Happiness and enjoyment certainly are factors, but nothing ever gets done if one contemplates the state of one's feelings as of primary moment, or allows them to dictate action. An over-long misery of helplessness can be very wearing, but it is possible to find a certain joy even in that, and the habit of endurance is worth paying a good deal for. I have paid for it pretty heavily, as God knows.

Looking back on it, my military ambitions were, from the first, ludicrously impossible. War, when you get it, is a matter of emergencies to be met instantly by that ready instinct which I never possessed. Again, war to the soldier is a very rare thing, but military life is above all things practical. The officer is the moral driving force to his sergeants and to his men. He also stands on a pedestal. He cannot possibly keep out of the way; impassivity is required of the men—it is no use at all to him. To the other cadets and to the officers it was probably obvious that I never would be a capable officer, but in those days there was no machinery of reports for getting rid of incapables so long as they passed examinations and did nothing involving a court martial.

It is odd that I never saw it myself. I was very fond of military science. I do not think I really understood it, but I also think I knew more of it than most, though less of if than the really capable. I gave it up, primarily because the opportunities of service were too few. The war of the gospel was unceasing. A parish mission at home (1878) decided me; for I imagined I saw there what that war of the gospel might be. My father said: 'You must finish,' and I did.

. . .

No further account of his conversion has been found, and we have no more than this to explain why he turned from a soldier into a priest. But it may be remembered that in 1878 the struggle between the great powers for colonial responsibilities was at its height; in this the issues were decided, not on the battlefield, but by diplomatic means on the basis of influences already established. This no doubt helped to turn the minds of military men towards educational and missionary problems.

II

I went to Oxford in 1879. I remember well the sigh of satisfaction with which, after passing my entrance, I sat down in my own room (at Queen's). It was my first introduction to happiness. I felt nothing like it when I went to Woolwich. I was, of course, very shy, but if I was afraid of society, men did not frighten me. I could go my own way in peace. I had a little circle of friends. They thought I was very clever; I knew they were very dense. In my time four years was the customary residence. I got through Smalls and Pass Moderations with some difficulty, and took Honour Moderations in Mathematics for the honour of Woolwich. I got a third. My mind and character were just what they had been in a child's boarding-school. Conversion in this respect made little change. Deafness was a tremendous factor, not however because it changed anything, but because it prevented my changing. As a child I had no necessity for knowing things or people, or therefore for getting on with them. As a boy I had no opportunity. As a young man, just when I might have escaped, I found myself suddenly walled in. I may note that at Oxford, and indeed until 1900 or so, I could follow lectures or sermons fairly. Till about 1920 I had not much difficulty in private conversation. I was only lost in company. In other words I might have friends, but they must come and see me. It was dangerous to go to them, as there might be other people there. But, if you do not go into company, and if you are nervous and uncomfortable when you are there, it is not easy to make friends.

At Oxford, I learnt two main things: (1) the width of God's world, and of His interest therein; (2) the habit of thinking. First, I found myself treated as a reasonable being. It is true that I was left to myself, but I was no longer frightened, and as I laid aside my armour, my mind began to expand. Secondly, I found something for it to expand over. While I was cramming up Xenophon's parasangs for my entrance with the aid of a crib (how else could one be expected to do Greek?) I read Kingsley's *Madam How and Lady Why*. It is the most fascinating book of 'Nature Studies' I know—every line of it as instinct with sound theology as with sound science.

28

I left the army at the urging of an intense Evangelical pietism. That I brought to Oxford. I joined the Evangelical group— Webster (afterwards of All Souls', Langham Place), and Mullins (of the Anglo-Continental Church Society). I do not think I interested them. They were not good at theories. There were theories of the Atonement, of course; they were somewhat crude. There was no formal world-theory. It worked out into a division of the world into converted and unconverted, saved and not-saved, with an ultimate heaven and hell objective. How far the leaders accepted the first antithesis I do not know. I did, and a good many did. I recognized the second consequence, but I think most of us were a little restless, and did not like to face it.

Kingsley's book broke into this narrow religionism like a revelation. I heard a voice crying, 'The earth is full of the glory of the Lord'—and then it told me of globigerina ooze and the formation of chalk. It was not to me bathos at all. It was the same voice saying, 'Look how God does things. Is it not lovely?' But then what had that got to do with being converted? Was conversion all that God cared for?

For a moment I dreamed of a gospel of science. I would do maths and astronomy and then take up science. Poor me! I presently saw that I did not know any maths and never should. Plain to see I had not brains enough, as I might have learnt long before. Leisure-wise, I tried to learn geology, but that also was too much for me. I never could remember—nor get to know—my minerals, and it was the same with fossils, except a few main types.

I remember laying it down as a rule—'Never let anything go by without having a shot at it.' I tried to learn the piano and took singing lessons. I read Ruskin, and attended his drawing school, as well as sports, which will do well enough as an instance. I learnt rowing at Oxford, because they were willing to coach you without expecting you to know it already, and it suited me well. There is a single stroke, difficult to acquire but always the same, with clear reasons. I became quite a decent oar.[1] It is impossible to begin cricket or football at Oxford. I tried hard to learn cricket

[1] During his first curacy he rowed in a crew of Oxford men from Dover to Calais, but was prostrate, though undefeated, when the boat arrived at the French coast.

at Ashton (when I was twenty-one) and tennis at thirty-five. They were all much too difficult for me. I had left off playing before I had really thought out the correct strokes; especially the first essential, to watch the ball fixedly till it actually comes on to the bat or racquet. You would suppose everybody knew that. I wonder if everybody does. I know I didn't.

I worked at all these things, according to opportunity, as seriously as if I had to make my living out of them. It struck me as odd how easily people gave in to the 'one-talent' feeling. People would not try sports, because they were 'not athletic,' nor study seriously, because they were 'not clever.' But it is so boring not to be getting on with something; it is also irreverent. If you have only one talent, the poor thing must work overtime if you are to get any profits—even if it cannot do the work of five talents.

Did I get on? I believe that, fairly uniformly, I succeeded in doing most things, except music, better than the people who did not 'go in' for doing them, though never as well as those who did. I was never good enough even for a second team, partly for lack of nerve, partly that my eyesight is not accurate, partly from general stupidity. There are a lot of nice things in God's world, and if I could not do them, nor shine at them, I got to understand them a bit, and to love them.

Meanwhile about my second year I began reading Maurice, who was a real thinker. Kingsley was not. Though he had given me matter for thought, he was too prejudiced and impatient. In thinking, I found something I could do, and I must explain what I mean by it, and what exactly it was that I learnt from Maurice, who is to my mind one of the profoundest thinkers who ever lived.

Thinking is, I suppose, concerned with meanings, and in meanings we see, or are looking for, the universal under the particular, the one under the many, the law under the instance, the cause in the effect, the permanent under the changing, the eternal under the temporal. The phrases may be logical, philosophical, scientific, or religious. One way or another you are finding your way to the how and the why. How does the right stroke go at tennis, and why is it right? The one is a simple rule; the other is a matter really of mathematics, partly of physiology. How are people converted? I suppose successful preachers could give you hints on how to succeed—some can tell you one thing, some another. A good many cannot tell you how it is they are so effective, but the methods mostly rest on psychology, sometimes on herd-psychology, the effect of surroundings, e.g. hymn-singing; sometimes on individual psychology, e.g. the effect of mere iteration, or of phrases which catch the mind.

All that is method, a matter of how. If you ask what is conversion, you go off into a much deeper region. What is a human soul, and in what relation does it, can it, ought it to stand to something else? If that relation is necessary to its life, why is it so difficult to find, or so often missed? Why does the soul shrink from it? Why is it so reluctant to 'turn back'? The mechanism of psychology may provide the meaning or way of certain changes in the soul; the latter questions are concerned with the meaning of the soul itself.

So far I stuck carefully to the word 'meaning'; there is an alternative; and most people would have found the above paragraphs easier to follow if I had said 'meaning or explanation.' I avoided it; for there is an exceedingly important difference. The thing means what it means, and its meanings stretch to all infinity. An explanation is so much of its meaning as you can give. You can explain chalk as a rock formed from globigerina ooze, dried and solidified. You can make shift to explain globigerina, drying, and solidification, though they are very tangled businesses; you will never get to the end of them, for at most you have not got more than fragments of the explanation. And then, if I ask you suddenly, 'And now, what is the meaning of chalk?' you can only bow your head and worship.

> And God said,
> let the dry land appear,
> and it was so.
> And God called the dry land Earth,
> and God saw that it was good.

The real confusion of life comes here in two forms. First of all, people do not realize the difference. Mostly, they are just so far reasonable that they like to have some sort of explanation, and they resent being asked to go further. There are two words which cover everything with a fascinating completeness. How does he do it? 'Oh, because he is *clever*.' The other is moral—Why does he, or mankind, do such things? Let us say, because he is *good*, religious, devout; or because they are *bad*.

The second form of confusion is the simple fact that people do not want to go further. The object of an explanation is to explain, and that means in effect to get rid of a troublesome question. People are not only perplexed at finding further questions. They are frightened at them, and proportionately annoyed at those who put them up. Of course they are well aware that others give explanations different from their own, and that too needs explaining; for we cannot admit we are not reasonable. But two universal explanations cover the difficulty. 'Does this other man agree with me?' If so, that he has found yet another explanation of my position is very clever on his part. Does he disagree? Then there is a moral reason for his palpable evasions. The pride, obstinacy, perversity of Romanisers, protestants, unbelievers, or parsons is well known, and the imputation of motive not difficult to justify.

Here Kingsley failed me. Certain things he saw very well: the many-sidedness of God's world, and of men's souls, i.e. of common souls. Some people he did not understand at all. Of course we were tossing various controversial questions to and fro. There was 'Ritualism,' but we knew little of it. I do not think a single man in our college genuflected. There was no 'Modernism,' but there was 'Broad Church.' It never appealed to me. And there was High Church. Farrar's *Eternal Hope* was still debated. Rome was only a distant factor. In Kingsley's hatred of Rome and High Church at the time I acquiesced . . . I may have felt Kingsley's inadequacy. Dimly I rather think I did, but I did not see clearly that he was making no attempt to understand them. He was sure that there was a moral obliquity on the part of the aforesaid.

With Maurice I was in a different atmosphere. All I have said above concerning the real essence of meanings is Maurice pure and simple. I do not remember that he gives any formal account of it, but it comes up repeatedly in his *Life,* and in scraps elsewhere. Quite definitely he taught me to look for the meaning of explanations. In that single phrase there were two sides. In the first place an explanation is a verbal statement. Now when Maurice has done it often enough for you, you may begin to see what a multitude

2

*The founder at
Vassall Road*

*The curate with his boys
at S. Barnabas,
Southfields*

3

*In the garden at
Mildenhall*

*With Fr. Woodward,
and the first students
(1894)*

of these explanations are merely verbal formulae, which may or
may not have once meant something, but are now simply counters
which have, quite probably, ceased to mean anything, but are still
handed about as the correct reply to arguments or questions.
Maurice taught me to go back to what the question really meant,
and what the formula really meant, in order to see whether one
answered the other or not.

The second side, implied by the 'reality' of a meaning, goes
far deeper than anything which might refer only to the uncer-
tainties and inadequacies of words. I can explain it best by a
favourite instance. Here are some Lutheran doctrines—Justification
by faith, or the sole authority of Scripture. You may think you
can prove their inadequacy, and Luther's own failure to explain
them consistently. All said and done, what did they mean to him?
You can get rid of that by the explanations of self-will and so on,
or, more sympathetically, that he was making a universal law out
of his own particular experience. Maybe he was: such things
have been done. I have done them myself. But how did Luther's
experiences, if they were only particular, create such a wide movement? Surely the approach to an answer must begin from this,
that men's souls were in need; that their needs were being, not
met, but stifled by a teaching and remedies which had no solid help
in them. Luther believed he had a gospel. He tried to explain
its meaning. People followed him because they found a help they
needed. There was a great deal that he did not understand; meanings for life, meanings in things he rejected. That was why many
people would not follow him; that was where his followers found
more difficulties: instead of meeting them they tried to cover them
up with artificial explanations exactly as those predecessors had
done against whom Luther protested.

Maurice is one of the most obscure of writers. I am reading his
Kingdom of Christ now, and it is almost maddening to see him
describing Lutheran developments without any exact quotation of
what they said, and without names or dates for the exact development he is dealing with (I wish someone who knew could provide
footnotes). Of course I was much too ignorant to know. Possibly for
me it was all the better. After all, I was not concerned with Luther-
anism. I was concerned with life, with my own soul, with the souls
of those about me. As I saw Maurice digging into a movement

C

in order to find its real meaning, partly expressed, partly hidden by the explanations given . . . I began digging too. I remember saying, 'When I have read two pages of Maurice I have forgotten what he said. I am thinking so furiously myself.'

Maurice's phrase was 'I am not so much interested in men's systems (doctrines or conclusions) as in their method.' So it was with Maurice himself. It was not his doctrines—I never saw that he had any special to himself—it was the way he reached them, and the use he made of them. By a method I do not think Maurice meant, certainly I did not, that digging was an interesting and healthy exercise in itself. The subsoil determines the character of the soil, and if you want to build on the rock, you must dig, and not be content with surface trenches. I was seeking the infinite truth of the creeds, as that which underlay life.

I spent three years thinking incessantly. I had found something which not even my stupidity and incapacity need prevent my doing. On the contrary it was these very defects which drove me to it. I could not get on with people. No, but I could watch them, and think about them, and many other things also. The process I call thinking was not exactly 'philosophy' in the technical sense; though I have known people call it that—I have used the word myself—for want of a better. It was some twenty-five years afterwards before I began to study philosophy in a formal way, and I find myself thinking about philosophy very much as I think over cricket, or mathematics, or history. I do not think the two are really the same, but philosophy is the thing that comes nearest to it, and I can say definitely that while in philosophy I can make out a good deal which is very useful to me, another good deal is beyond my powers. I have not got the brains nor the subtlety of mind to be really a philosopher, but I can do 'thinking' (whatever it is) better than most people, because I am always doing it.

Beyond a certain facility at thinking, acquired by incessant practice, self-consciousness is the only faculty which I believe I possess in a somewhat exceptional degree. Whether it is a natural gift, or whether it is only a result of being so much driven in upon myself, I do not know any one so continuously aware of exactly what he is doing or wants to do, of his own motives and feelings at any moment. I daresay many people can do it much better, but for thinking purposes it is exceedingly useful. If you can always analyse yourself, you can see how a good many things are done. You can reproduce an act, or the tone of man's voice, in your imagination and see what feelings go with it.

After I had been reading Maurice for a year or so, I finished with maths; for it was plainly no use to go on with that. I could not read Greats (philosophy); for you were expected to read all Plato and Aristotle in Greek. The same sort of demands forbade my taking theology. History remained the only subject, and I thought it would suit me very well.

Ultimately I just read. One thing I did learn was the art of rapid reading. . . . I had never learnt to take notes. I just sucked everything in, noting its bearings. If I wanted it, I expected it to stick. If it slipped out, I reckoned it might go. 'Memory?' No, I have no memory for words, but if I have thought and understood a thing, it becomes part of my mind, and that does not slip out.

I was thinking, and I did think, but my thinking was much ahead of my knowledge. I had a profound belief that history was a drama of the purposes of God. I had not the least inclination to suppose that, because our history was concerned with politics and constitutions and nationalities and such like, it was just a sideshow in God's mind. When Popes, clergy, moralists—in history or in our own day—have treated it so, tried on that ground to take the superior attitude, they seemed to me frankly unbelieving. That was what I had learnt from Kingsley. On the other hand, just for this reason, I was making dives for ultimates long before I knew how to make a solid road out of my facts. At the same time, I knew and had learnt from science that that was what had to be done. I had undertaken a job about fifteen sizes too big for a mind in most ways too slow. Odd times I could do essays which (I believe) my tutor thought distinctly good. If I make a guess, I fancy he put me down as a probable third, with a possible second, if I was in luck, would stick to my work, and leave theology alone. My friends (poor dears) thought I would get a first. I said, 'I might. I should dearly love to. It would be screamingly funny. The next funniest thing would be to get a fourth. I bet on the fourth.' I had made a frantic rush covering whole centuries in the last term, and I was tired. I could no nothing but write generalities. I got a fourth. I believe I trembled on the edge of a third.

III

By 1883 my mind was as much formed as that inchoate thing is ever likely to be. What was I to do with it? A fourth in history may or may not have provided an adequate estimate of my intellectual powers, but it was not sufficient to open the door to a university career. The old evangelical idea of rushing out to convert people was gone. There was a gospel, but I had a good deal to learn first. My father wanted me to come to Manchester, but I would not go where he was. First, I was not at all sure—even then—that I could walk in his steps; and secondly he was a canon of the cathedral, and I did not think it was playing the game to use his influence.

I ought to have gone to Cuddesdon, to learn the elements of my business. I had never heard of the place, or of the idea. If I had, I might have become a quite decent third-rate curate. I might also have got to know somebody, which is very useful (as will appear), and to know how to live with people, which is still more useful. As things were, all I knew was that I had an enormous amount of thinking and reading to do. I would go into the country. Where? They were all the same to me. So I blundered into a parish five miles from Maidstone. We had monthly communion, but we did a goodish deal of visiting. I had a weekly sermon, joined the London Library, and got books by fifteen volumes at a time.

I used to keep a sort of account book of this reading, entering books and number of pages, week by week. In 1884 I read about ninety books of all sorts, philosophy, art, poetry, six novels, commentaries. I started to work through the Fathers, beginning with the sub-apostolic—more of my absurd 'research' work—but I soon saw that I ought to begin with Plato. During these two years I read most of the short dialogues, and wrote my own introductions to them. I had learnt at Oxford, and continued here, the habit of 'working.' I do not mean that I was not often idle and self-indulgent, but I had got rid of that strange idea of a 'pastime.' When I could get tennis or cricket, I worked at them. When I read a novel, I thought about it. I recognized the difference between stiff books, which needed notes, and easy books which you could read straight through, and that at meals you must only read the latter. But reading fatuous stuff, when you could get good stuff, simply bored me. I do not like being bored. I like to feel that something is getting on. The effort of philosophy or science is considerable; you may not always be equal to it, but if you can follow it, it is much more interesting than meaninglessness. From Oxford onwards, I have worked holidays and all other days. The attempt to separate 'work' and enjoyment seems to me the superstition of schoolboys.

I continued reading, more or less in this fashion, until Vassall Road. I shall have to admit then how little had come of it, for want of method, especially in regard to any formed knowledge. But in other ways a good deal has come of it. At Oxford I stuck to what I wanted, and let the rest go, but I had a better way of putting it: I called it 'manuring the soil.' Crowds of students can make nothing of the significance of what they are supposed to be learning, because they have no experience of what folks do or think. I got my experience by reading books of all kinds.

Here is a parable: you have to get home with your barrow (whether theology or parishes, roots of things or fruits, is of no moment). It is a bit overloaded, and you must rest at intervals. That is all right. Boss pays full time. But you may as well make your stops where there are sticks or other bits—kindling maybe—to pick up, so that even the rests are not wholly waste.

So, like Dick Whittington, I went to London with a vague idea of doing something. The Archbishop sent me to Canon Mason, who was running a sort of brotherhood of mission priests at Trinity Square. Mason looked me over, and knew at once he could do nothing with such a half-baked animal. I wasted a few months at Toynbee Hall. They also were not impressed. Then I began looking for a curacy. To-day (1929) cooks and curates have a golden time. Either need only wave a dish-cloth or a dog-collar, then mistresses and vicars tumble over one another, imploring you to have pity on them. I was ordained on the top of the wave, and vicars could afford to be particular. I have no account of exactly how many turned my application down.

At last I was taken on by Hassard, a very capable man (after-

wards a canon of Truro) at Holy Trinity, Dalston. He was somewhat doubtful (no wonder). A few weeks later, before I was
licensed, he met a really capable man, and, somewhat shame-
facedly, told me he was the man he had been wanting. I told him
straight out that his first duty was to the Church, and to his parish.
If another man was better, it was his duty to take him, and mine
to clear out. It seemed to me plain sense. Someone once said to
me: 'But he ought not to have done it, all the same.' I do not
in the least see why. I had a few weeks to find another market.
The importance of this little episode is that Hassard was by way
of being a Catholic. We had choral masses. The ideas I had
learnt from Maurice. It was the first time I ever saw Catholicism
at work. It carried me on a long way.

This time without much trouble I found another curacy at
S. Paul's, Wimbledon Park (with S. Barnabas, Southfields), and
I must say more about it, because it constitutes my one real experience of parish work. It was a new High Church parish, between
Wimbledon and Wandsworth, which were both Low Church.
Earl Beauchamp was our father-founder. There is a range of very
swell houses facing Wimbledon Common, of which we were
allowed a very small bite (about two hundred people), with as
much more of a congregation as we could poach. There was a
brick cowshed as a temporary parish church, and a very nice
vicarage. Before I left, we had half built a very fine church. We
never got beyond Mattins, and a white stole on festivals.

Among the meadows by the Wandle were some fifteen hundred
artisan to slum folk in a set of small, mostly jerry-built, houses,
two families to a house. They were mine. I had a small tin-
tabernacle, holding about a hundred and fifty. On Sundays I had
to assist at Mattins, but I had an eight a.m. celebration of my own,
and evensong. There was no parish-room, but after a year or so
I took a house of my own, knocked the downstairs rooms together
and made shift.

So far as 'the Park' was concerned I was simply 'the curate.'
They were moderately civil, and I got occasional invitations to
tennis, and some other spiritual functions, but I knew nothing of
society. That is of no moment, but I was desperately shy and
frightened. They saw I was nobody, and gave me the go-by. At

first I preached occasionally, but they petitioned that the curate should not preach. Practically I never did. I was trying to preach from notes. I think I was also trying to reach to the best of my thoughts, which is a great error. If you really are a brilliant preacher, old or young, I suppose people will take anything. But people do not like original ideas at any time, and certainly not from the young. Moral: as in rock-climbing, in ticklish places always keep well inside what you can do. I did not really care: I was mildly amused at it all. It is only to be mentioned that among these people were the Hollands, and I got to know Scott Holland—the only great person I ever got to know till I came on Willie Temple, and, in a lesser degree, a few others—who are all bishops now, but that belongs to this century.

I gave my life to my people. I meant to win the whole parish to the love of God. I knew very little of real priestly work, or of parochial methods, but the intentions were not lacking. Why did it not answer? Why do clergy slack? An immense number do. Not a few fill up real slackness with fussiness and organizations. I was very different to most, and yet I think I can answer. It is the sense of helplessness and failure. No one slacks over what he can really do. The ordinary parson fails for want of thinking. Perhaps none of us have really thought out what the Gospel means in the common life of the common layman. We know, at most, only our own spiritual life. Crowds of us fail, because we have got our ideals in the wrong order. Machinery, clubs, etc., are a useful means of 'getting hold' of people. Then congregations, services, numbers of communicants, seem to be necessary means to the true end, which is godliness of life. But when we treat these very visible means as immediate ends, they obscure both to us and to our people the true end, which is so little visible, and so hard to estimate. If we kept that godliness of life in the foreground, it might bring all its means with it as its natural expression.

'But if I knew these things, why did I not do them?' First, I did not know them. I was not in the least at home in, master of, confident of, my own thoughts. Even now I could not do it. Batting is, after all, a very practical matter. The genius does it by instinct. The fifth-rate player tries to do it in the same way, and cannot. He would improve his class a good deal, if he would

39

study the science a bit. I quite admit that you cannot make runs by science. The pith of success is always eyesight, nerve, readiness of action, and I have never had any of these things. When I had learnt to trust my thoughts, I could sometimes be quite effective. But the little daily business, planting and hoeing, is done on the surface. Thinking is a kind of digging. To my mind, the practical person fails because he does not dig into the reasons of things. I was, have been, am a failure because I can do nothing else.

Is the ordinary parson a failure? I think he succeeds less, and I often think he fails less, than very often he and we suppose. There is an enormous amount of 'godliness' which never finds expression. If it is so, it is kept alive by the unrecognized work of the Church and its clergy as a whole force.

Was I a failure? Before I left, Southfields had been set up with a railway and a station. It took a year or two before houses began to appear. Now there is a dense population of fifteen thousand and a big church. As for my work, I have heard people say that my memory and inspiration did something or other—I have forgotten what. I am sure it is very gratifying to believe that one's work was not all failure. Personally I have no such gratifying belief, but it may have been so. God knows I did mean well, and God somehow can make use even of the feeblest souls.

IV

NOTE

Theological education in 1890, so far as the Church of England was concerned, meant primarily some immediate professional preparation for the pastoral office. This might be done in three ways by graduates, who still formed the great majority of Anglican ordinands (the proportion in England and Wales in 1874 was 461 : 194).[1] Either (1) they might go to live with a clergyman, some of whom, like Dr. Vaughan, had a deserved reputation for training 'doves'; or (2) they might remain at the university, attending theological lectures from the professors of divinity; or (3) they might attend a theological college, where in most cases they would study with a certain number of students who had not graduated.[2] Only a few of them had read theology for the B.A. degree. The theological tripos at Cambridge and the school of theology at Oxford were relatively recent innovations,[3] and the ground covered in them was limited to Biblical studies and the first four centuries of church history. The theological colleges covered a wider ground, with much variety. While some were committed to a party, others played for safety. None of them had time to go very deep, for the graduates, if they came at all, stayed little more than a year, and often less. The rest had commonly a hard struggle to acquire the tools for making a bare beginning in their theological studies.

A predominantly graduate ministry is not necessarily a class ministry, but circumstances in the nineteenth century made it increasingly difficult for any but the wealthiest classes to support their sons at Oxford and Cambridge, even with the aid of foundation scholarships. First of all the wealthy, both the landowners and the men of business, had come to attach an increasing importance to university education for their children, in a competitive world where mere patronage could no longer secure a living, and a world of action where leisured gentlemen were nothing like so content to live without a profession as they had been

[1] F. W. B. Bullock, *A History of Training for the Ministry, 1800–74*, Budd and Gillat, St. Leonard's-on-Sea, 1955, p. 144. The graduates are reckoned as those from Oxford, Cambridge, Dublin, and Durham. The proportion in 1841 from the same universities was 558 : 48.

[2] Ibid., p. 147.

[3] See A. F. Hort, *Life of F. J. A. Hort*, 1896, vol. 1, pp. 367–8, for Hort's criticism of the Cambridge tripos, introduced in 1854.

41

in the eighteenth century.[4] *As a result of this the cost of living in the older universities had risen sharply. The poor scholar had become an exceptional figure, whose struggle to live was harder than ever. Church patronage, once commonly given to dependants, or to a clever lad from the village, was now bestowed on family friends and kinsfolk, partly because families were larger and more anxious for some responsible employment, but also because the value of ecclesiastical preferments had on the whole risen through agricultural improvements. But in the last quarter of the century agricultural depression brought about a steep decline in clerical incomes, and with it a decline in the supply of graduate candidates for ordination, accentuated by the intellectual crisis that followed the publication of* The Origin of Species *in 1859 and* Essays and Reviews *in 1860. The Church of England once more began to look for recruits to the lower middle class, who had furnished a large proportion of her ministry in the seventeenth and eighteenth centuries, and, with more hesitation, to the working classes, whose abilities were revealed by the extension of elementary education. But the means were now lacking to educate these men either for, or at, the universities. The grammar schools, with important exceptions, had been transformed into public schools for the wealthier classes after the pattern of Dr. Arnold's reforms at Rugby. Moreover the improved status of the ministry in the purely social scale in the nineteenth century had made ordination an attraction to those who wished to rise in the world. This was a sound reason for looking with some distrust on attempts to recruit clergy from the lower classes, inside or outside the universities.*

The one possible answer lay in the revival of the idea of a sacrificed ministry, devoted to the cause of God without any thought of promotion or preferment, of pay or comfort. In the mission field this was absolutely and undeniably necessary, at a time when Africa and India took a heavy toll in life and health from all who went out to serve there. But to the discerning the need was equally obvious in every part of industrial England and Wales, where the working classes, despite all the effort and energy which churchmen had given to the increase and improvement of elementary education, were in their adult years almost wholly alienated from a Church which seemed to belong to the upper and middle classes. To meet this need it was above

[4] Bullock, in op. cit., p. 143, argues that in 1800 a considerable majority of university graduates were candidates for the ministry, and calculates the proportion in 1874 as 35%. In the eighteenth century gentlemen, as distinct from noblemen, did not go to the university unless they contemplated ordination. They completed their education in the Inns of Court, as in Elizabethan times. (See e.g. *II Henry IV*, Act 3, sc. 2.)

LAY VOCATION

all things necessary to put first things first, not the supply of clergy, but the supply of servants of the Church, ready to go anywhere to do what was needed, without any promise of promotion, without choice of work, without marriage, without pay. Among these, if they could be recruited, priests, teachers, and doctors might all be found, as well as other helpers. But no one will make such a sacrifice unless he sees the vision of the gospel, meditates deeply upon it, understands it in his heart. To this end theological education, spiritual discipline, the deepening of the devotional life are all necessary. None of them will go very far without the rest.

The following papers were written long after the events which they describe. In one respect they may mislead. Fr. Kelly's emphasis was not at the beginning on training for the ordained ministry, but on education for the divine service. The 'three conditions' (p. 45) pointed to the possibility of ordination for at least some, but many would be lay helpers of varying kinds. All however must 'learn how to think their faith.' Only at a later stage did it become clear that while a Religious Community can make use of men in a great variety of tasks, and those who have not the vocation to life in community can be trained for the dedicated life of the priesthood under religious discipline, only in very special cases was it possible for missions and parishes (apart from Communities) to employ laymen under the conditions of poverty and celibacy.

In about 1888 a good deal of attention was given to the possibility of using paid lay readers 'in view of . . . the undesirability of increasing the number of ordained clergy, many of whom can never hope to become incumbents.' [5] The S.P.C.K. started a college in Stepney for training men for this purpose in 1896, and it is interesting to notice that, when this was first projected, Fr. Kelly applied for a post on the staff (probably in 1890).[6] 'The demand for readers was in excess of the supply, and after a year's training the salary offered was £75 in London and other large cities, and £65 in the country.' By 1903 over two hundred of these were at work in some lay capacity, and twenty had been ordained. But 'by 1912 the resident students had fallen to sixteen and it was becoming hard to place them.' [7] This throws some light on a like problem. If readers trained for a year were a problem to parish priests with more general education but no more professional training, lay helpers theologically educated for four years were as hard or harder to use, either at home or overseas.

[5] W. K. Lowther Clarke, *A History of the S.P.C.K.*, 1959, p. 162.
[6] According to his introduction to the *Annual Reports of S.S.M.*
[7] As 5.

43

In those days—the 1880s—when curates were much more common than they are now, every part of the Church, notably the mission field, was crying out for men.[8] Where were they to come from? Those recruited through the usual channels were insufficient to meet the new demands. In my second curacy, in south London, I tried to do what I could with the boys in the poor district of Southfields. It seemed to me that the Church could find the men she needed from such as these, if only the necessary education could be provided. I went to Scott Holland, the only man I knew among the big people, and suggested that if a free college was started, with no half-baked gentility, we might get quite a number; but who was I to start anything? He said it was coming, but not yet. (The result proved that he was quite wrong.) I was ready to give myself, and what money I had, for anything.

During 1890 I worked out in my head the idea of what I wanted, but I had no notion how or by whom it could be carried out. There were at that time three openings for just myself. One was in the north of England, and another in Australia (where I might be of some use, being no scholar); but the third was the most pressing. An ex-naval chaplain, Bishop Corfe, had been offered the bishopric of Korea, for which a big grant had been allotted. The intention was to do the job on the lines of U.M.C.A., with a common fund, no marriage, and a community mission. This, I knew, would be for me useless than anything, for I was much too stupid to learn a language, and much too full of ideas to be a useful missionary. However, I took the alternatives to Scott Holland, and asked him to make the choice. He told me to go to Korea—the one thing I did not want to do.[9] But he had said it, and so I had to go.

After looking round for the best part of a year, Bishop Corfe had found one deacon to go with him. When I told him of my dreams, he told me that he had a dozen young laymen who were willing to go, and asked me to take charge of them. Here was a

[8] S.S.M., Q.P., December, 1950.
[9] In the introduction to the *Annual Reports of S.S.M., 1891–1910* there is a touch of detail that is absent here. 'Walking down the Strand to a Purity Society Meeting at Exeter Hall, on the steps he chose the latter' (Korea). 'With a heavy heart I wrote to the Bishop (or his Commissary) the same night. It may have been May 19th.'

wonder: just as I gave it up, the whole idea was thrust back into my hand. I say the *whole,* my passion being always for a whole; I had already thought out in its wholeness what a 'Society' ought to be and how it ought to work. As regards the Korean Brotherhood, it was as clear to me then as it is now that it should have been made on the spot where recruits were wanted. Obviously they were not there but in this country. I said at once: 'The first business of your college is to test. You cannot work a testing house without a back door on the street, and it is no good taking a man to Korea, finding him a failure, and leaving him on the beach at Chemulpho. You must test them here.' I was sent to Brooke, vicar of S. John the Divine, Kennington, the bishop's commissary. We proceeded to look over the men, and I said to Brooke: 'If I can scare them off, I have done the first part of my business.' So I saw them one after another, and of the dozen two agreed to come. Brooke and I took a house in Vassall Road, just opposite the church.

Always running in my head nowadays is the famous saying from Newman's 'Lead, kindly Light': 'I do not ask to see the distant scene; one step enough for me.' I could never make out what the difficulty is; but every one says, 'How true!' To my mind, to start with, it isn't true. What is the good of taking a single step if you don't know which way you are going and what you are making for? It would seem to be very absurd for the unknown curate, without anybody to back him, to be starting with an image picture of an S.S.M. bigger than we have to-day, when really there were just two ignorant boys and his ignorant self. I have always thought that the title of 'Founder' should belong to Bishop Corfe or Canon Brooke; for, though I had the idea, they had the practical courage to make it possible. When Brooke took me over the house he had found for us, he said in ecstasies: 'This will give you room to expand. We could get eight men in it!' I reminded him of this when I showed him Kelham.

I had now formulated a scheme [10]: 'You have any number to choose from. Make them choose themselves, on THREE CONDITIONS. (1) We do not offer ordination (to many it is just a means to pious gentility). Ask them simply to give their lives to

[10] *Ad filios.*

45

the Divine Service. (2) No pay: Korea, like U.M.C.A., is a community mission. (3) By consequence, no marriage. We can't ask a binding promise. We must be content with an honest intention. Next, the life must so correspond as to make sacrifice a reality. Finally, we must have a real four-year education. Men must learn how to think their faith. With all this useful material, we shall yet have a house of hundreds, and it will come to a Religious Society.'

Brooke, as commissary, was our superior and took us on. We rented an ugly house at Brixton to hold eight men. The fun began. We opened on January 1st, 1891 with two, and another directly appeared. Most of the year drew blank, but a letter in *The Church Times* brought sixty applications—eleven were accepted. The U.M.C.A. joined and took six. Of the eleven, six more disappeared before the day, but now the fun began in earnest.

We furnished the house in our own fashion—wooden chairs, deal tables, iron beds, and cooking irons.[11] We had a small room for an oratory. I will describe our life at once, for it changed little for many years. We began with Prime and Mattins at six, and after a short interval—time enough to do our rooms—we went to the Celebration in Church at 7 a.m. Thence back to breakfast, which we managed ourselves. It was a plain bread and butter breakfast, with jam, I admit. Then began the housework. One man was responsible for accounts, one for washing up, and one swept the stairs. They changed rounds monthly. At 9 a.m. we had Terce, and then worked till dinner at 1.30 p.m. with Sext at 12 noon. None was at 2 p.m., tea at 6 p.m.—bread and butter as before; Evensong in Church at 7 p.m., and Compline at 9.30 p.m. Silence was kept till Sext next day. It was years after—I forget how long—before we learnt to divide the silence into a Greater, or absolute silence, up to Terce, and a Lesser, from all talk other than about work, up to Sext. It was not a very well organized day, but we managed. Saturday was scrubbing day. Canon Brooke found us a most delightful old lady, Mrs. Staples, a true servant of God, who would come and cook for us.

---

[11] *An Idea in the Working*, pp. 17–18 (rearranged).

We began with a month's holiday a year.[12] After a year or two we gave three holidays, as we do now, and in 1893 got a little football by walking two and a half miles. I began to play at thirty-three. I do not know why we did not all break down, but in fact our health was as good as it is now (1921) or better.

During those five years we had an odd succession of tutors, none of them very effective, and one or two curates helped. It was a difficulty that I had done no constructive theology, no church history after A.D. 180, no real dogmatics. I had to work my own way dragging the classes with me, but we never got better work out of the men; which was odd, for the spiritual state was mad. Men quarrelled endlessly, made parties, scamped the rules. Little as I knew of theology, I knew less of men. I never could understand men's ignorance of the English language. It always puzzles me now. For Christ and His Church they had given up personal ambitions and status, but they thought of nothing else. They promised to obey the rules, and never kept them. I believe that most of them were sincere, honest, truthful, yet they accepted principles, and were angry at being asked to carry them out. Truthful, they would not tell the truth; honest and sincere, they behaved dishonestly and insincerely.

If I had had the pluck of a mouse, I'd have told them to play up or go. But I believed they were sincere in their own way, and I had a weird belief that you can do anything if you go on. (You can't.) In explanation, everything has come to me by way of thinking. I thought myself out of Protestantism (never, thank God, out of evangelicalism). Before Southfields, I was a fortnight at a High Mass church on approval, but I had never otherwise seen Catholicism till I went to S. John's. It is to me always more a faith than a system.

I knew no one worth knowing in Catholic circles, and the few I did know were not very helpful, since to them 'the authority of the Church' was always apt to mean a series of doctrines stated by a recognized authority.[13] The idea of a Catholic Church and of Catholic authority made an immense appeal to me. It was a vision of a great, ordered, common Truth, wherein men at all times

[12] *Ad filios.*   [13] *Personal Thoughts Concerning Unity.*

47

lived: One God, One Faith. Protestantism with its talk of private judgment ceased to appeal to me. That I am a little private individual making my own way is a fact, but it is not a basis of faith. My faith lies beyond myself, in a Universal Truth which is God's Spirit. Certainly the phrase 'Scripture as interpreted by Catholic consent' seemed to come as near the truth as any phrase can. I would never separate myself from that consent, but Pusey's apparent belief that the teaching of God's Spirit could be fixed by a catena of consentual extracts, seemed to me to break down in fact as it does in principle. I could never be a Roman, because that theory is a formal substitution (vicariate) of another process for the living God. I am a learner. I wanted to learn from an eternal Spirit of all ages—primitive, medieval, modern—the self-same Spirit. If any one asked, but 'what do you learn?' I reply, two things primarily:

    (1) to believe in God, the infinite;

    (2) to distrust myself, the smallest of the small.

There is the beginning of my attitude to Reunion. All sectarianisms alike seem to lie in an evasion of these *principles* of faith, in an attempt to get away to something determined, to a process of determining. It is a parallel to the moralist's effort to fix 'good,' which is God, into a standard of right and wrong. It is S. Paul's antithesis of faith and law. After all, the 'determined' thing— be it doctrine or system—is an 'idol,' and God is an infinite life. I am not an iconoclast. We need images—dogmas and institutions —God has given them; but to make them equivalents for God, as though God were summarized in them, is idolatry.

There was a second thing. Faith is not only of thinking; it is of worship. The Athanasian Creed identifies it with worship. I had learnt a certain dread of 'pietism.' Just as I had learnt to see how easily faith in God might be confused with the acceptance of doctrines, so I had learnt as an Evangelical to see how easily it could be confused with devotional feeling. It was just here that the sacramental faith appealed to me, for the very essence of it was that a presence, an Act, a Gift of God, were set before you in act and fact, an object of faith, or understanding, and a ground of feeling, but not constituted by either. My priesthood could not lie in some cleverness or devoutness of my own; it was given by an appointed act in the order of God.

4

The first chapel at
Vassall Road

The chapel at Mildenhall.

5. *The great chapel at Kelham, built in 1928*

EDUCATION

I was just thirty, and had been doing parish work for some six years, when in 1890 I was set to my life work. I was to start a college which would train for the ministry young men with no money and with no special education. Therewith I came out into the world—so far as I was temperamentally capable of doing it. There were already several colleges of the same kind, and whether they were 'High Church' or 'Low Church,' the ideas and systems were much the same. Because the men were uneducated, the intellectual side must be simplified as much as possible. A few simple textbooks, giving the really essential facts of doctrine, must be got up. For explanations the student, unaccustomed to reading, must depend mainly on his lecturers. That he shall know at least the main facts, know which are the correct doctrines, and the reasons for them, is all you can expect. For the simple priest all this intellectual business is very secondary. It is not likely that he will come across many clever people. The one thing that really matters is the sincerity of his devotional life. (For some reason the intellectual life in a Protestant college is on a far higher, the devotional life on a far lower level than in Anglican colleges.)

I was expected to follow the customary system. I never dreamt of doing so. Educationally it was a hopeless system, but, what concerned me infinitely more, it was hopelessly at variance with all those theological principles which I have tried to describe. These men were going to be teachers of a faith, given in a Creed. This is said to be correct, and that incorrect, but I do not care about these words. I would rather ask, why is this doctrine vital, and that fatal, to a man's soul and capacity to live? Someone said it was, and he ought to know. Very well, we must go to him, and find out why he found it so; then each man must look into his own soul, find in his own life its questions and perplexities, its difficulties and diversities. There was no severance between chapel and lectures, as between devotionalism and intellectualism. Prayer is meditation, and study is meditation, but God, the love of God, the following of God, is one. At a later stage we summarized it under the term, 'theological football.' Here is a creed, a faith, a theology, a belief in God, and here is a boy's game. What have they to do with one another? Here is a cheese-factory, and here a cheese shop. Is God interested in the efficiency of our processes of manufactur-

49

D

ing and selling, or only in the morals of those who manufacture and sell? Surely, if God made the world, then our processes are efficient where they follow God's ways. If we split life into religious sections, moral sections, business sections, it is plain God does not; nor does He make that possible for most people.

For just these reasons we did not make any severance of study and 'practical work,' such as preaching or visiting. Indeed it seemed to us wrong that a student should be set to teach others before he had learnt to understand himself. Theology I conceive to be the study of the vision, of the great life-purpose, and there is no ultimate purpose except in God. If our theology is unpractical, it is that view of life-purpose that we have missed. It is possible that we have missed 'theology,' and are only studying 'theological subjects.' Then we had better get back. No doubt theology does need practice. Meditation, prayer, study, which all lead towards a vision of purpose; worship, scrubbing stairs, sweeping a passage, washing dishes, which flow from it, are all very appropriate passages at this stage, and useful at some other stages.

At Oxford, while lecturers were tracing the development of our glorious constitution, my mind was asking what God thought of it all. I found no answer. Now I had to find one. How God led His world, how men sought Him, were found by Him, how and where they missed Him, as we might; what their philosophies, their politics meant to them; how God used all things. I was desperately ignorant, but these were the essential things we had to seek.

We only gave one lecture a day. There were no textbooks to be got up, but all the books best worth reading—orthodox or heterodox. There was time to read and think, to get bewildered and to find a way through. There is no *right* of private judgment; there is a *duty* of learning. There is no right of thinking for oneself; there are a thousand ways of escaping it, and picking up easy phrases without thinking. It is fatally easy to teach men to love, and to argue about, opinions. You can do it by teaching them which are the 'correct' opinions; you can do it by inviting them to form their own opinions, and in other ways. It is extremely difficult to get people to see that anything wants thinking about. The infinity of God's ways none of us cares very much to face. I take it there are two essential principles of education, first, a profound reverence for the infinity of truth, secondly, a mingled honesty as to what one has learnt, and humility as to its inadequacy. And they are just the principles of faith in God. As to students, 'they shall all be taught of God,' for what you can really learn is what God gives you to see, but you must not think it is all there is. As to tutors, 'That which thou sowest is not quickened except it die, and thou sowest not that body which shall be, but God giveth it a body as it hath pleased Him.' I accepted, I would have them accept, the faith of the Catholic Church, but I never thought of that faith as a matter of opinions . . .

I taught some Scripture, but after the first year I gave that up to others, more learned and more competent. My part was history. In the third year I had to start doctrine. In the meanwhile I had been studying the *Summa* of S. Thomas Aquinas. In a sense it was to me a quite new side of things. Reality is always a certain infinite, therefore truth is infinite. Nevertheless what we learn are notions, or opinions, and it was with notions, opinions, ideas, that S. Thomas was dealing. What fascinated me in S. Thomas was his tremendous reverence for ideas, the infinite pains he took to define, to make clear, exactly what the thought, what each idea, was, exactly where it fitted in, honestly and consistently, with other thoughts. If any one asks whether I agreed with S. Thomas's opinions, or conclusions, I hardly thought of the matter in that light. I learnt from him that ideas too had a reality, that they should be handled very reverently; I learnt something of the method by which it could be done.

If I had not been a student of Maurice, I might have become a scholastic. As it was, as soon as I had worked out what I could of S. Thomas, I began to come back to my actualities, and it was about 1900 that, in working up my Church history course, I had to get down seriously to S. Augustine and his Predestinarianism. I never in my life had the least inclination to what is called Calvinism. Indeed, I thought, and still think, that Augustine's and Calvin's habit of treating Predestination as concerned primarily with the salvation or loss of particular souls was, in every possible direction, hopelessly misleading. God's will is always primarily the universal will, though of course it covers the individual, even the individual sparrow. God so loved the Cosmos, the whole world-order, that He gave His Only-Begotten Son.

It has always seemed to me an amazing thing that so many Christian people should regard the Predestinarian question as a merely academic problem, on the avowed ground that we are only concerned with what we have to do. We are concerned with what most matters, and that is not us and our doings. It has always seemed to me that Predestination, the doctrine of a Purpose and an over-ruling Power of God over all life, is the true central point to which all Dogmatic Theology leads up, from which all Ascetic (practical) Theology leads down. The Creed is in three parts: (a) What is God? What is an Infinite Will? There cannot be a world-order except around that Will. But how can man come to it? It is plain he cannot, but (b) there is a Gospel telling us that God came to man, and took this World-Order to Himself, redeemed it, not as we always think, by 'what He does,' but by what He suffered, —and out of that made Triumph and Ascension. (c) But, inasmuch as we are separate beings, with independent wills, choices, judgments, what have we, or can we have, in a common Redemption? How is this Infinite Will, Eternal and Universal, related to the Individual Will?

The attempt to split off fundamental questions as merely philosophical or intellectual, and to regard personal morality, piety, 'religion,' as the really vital factor, was putting ourselves before God. It involved splitting religion, *pietismus,* off into a sphere of its own for a clique of pious people. The common laity might understand the worship of God; they do not appreciate the worship of 'religion' as a personal state. All that I had first learnt from Kingsley, his broad interest in a nature-world, and in rough people. What I learnt from Maurice of the reality of God, from Catholicism of the reality of worship, from Augustine, of God's Will, purposing before all ages that Redemption in Christ for which man was made, was one whole lesson.

In human life, therefore, there are two ends, ideals, kingdoms, always at war—God and the self; the Eternal for which we are made, and the Temporal, in which we live—the Universal, which is Truth, and the particular, the fragmentary, which we are. Since there is this dissonance in us, its reconciliation lies only in God.

But we may know our littleness, and in confession and penitence, in humility, which is faith, there is love which is reconciliation and peace. Aquinas saw the complexity of ideas, but with all his power, I think he never realized that infinite complexity in human life which its inherent dissonance involves. I do not think that it could be realized by any mere sifting of ideas, since our life is in fact a dualism, an opposition, of two ideas. God understands; they come together in Him, not in anything we can explain or do. They come together in Christ, in the cross; they are reconciled in the Ascension. And something of unity is given to us by His Spirit, as we are able to bear it. All human life is a dualism.

Just after this (1902) I began to study psychology. From history, and by watching men's minds, I had learnt a great deal of the complexity of men's actual thinking, and of the importance of the subconscious, which was not at that time accepted doctrine. To make a comparison, just as Aquinas had taught me all that was possible in the way of sifting out the implications of an idea, so my psychology books gave me an opportunity for following the actual processes at work in men's minds.

Practical psychology [14] I had studied in my own way ever since I was an undergraduate, and I had formed a very definite idea of sub-conscious processes, first from watching my own mind ('unconscious cerebration' was a recognized nineteenth century phrase), and secondly from watching other people's minds, and how little they knew of the, often perfectly obvious, reasons on which they were going. I think it was about 1900 that someone gave me a book of Sidis, where the whole thing was worked out with experiments. . . . I had been wanting it for years. I also read James, who put me up to the sensation part. Then I wrote the psychology lectures about 1902. It is rather odd that when I got two Cambridge dons (one very eminent) to look at them, they declined to touch the subconscious part at all. It was just before Freud.

It was about 1907 that Neville Talbot insisted that I must get on terms with modern philosophy and read Kant. I spent six weeks accordingly; then went on to some books on Hegel, and tried James (*Pragmatism*). Certainly it was most essential. I admit that

[14] *Autobiography.*

a great deal of philosophic writing simply puzzles me. I am not greatly interested to know what a clever man can do with a theory. I do want to know what it is doing with him, and will do with other people when he and they use it. I want most of all to know what it can do for me. From what I could understand I built up an epistemology. I got a real conception of what 'knowledge' meant, and that gave me a secure foothold for my theology.

Whatever my intellectual defects may have been, and they were sufficiently grave to make it quite impossible that I should find a place in higher education, at least they saved me from trying to take our men by a road they could not possibly travel. Perhaps they enabled me to find a road by which such men *could* travel.

There were and are certain accepted axioms. Thinking is quite obviously the business of scholars; not all, even of them, made much pretence to do it. No one else should be allowed to do it at all. It is enough for the uneducated if they are taught the bare elements of scholarship, and a few of its attainments, rather as if where a man will never read Latin, he might at least know the declensions. Doctrine in a good many theological or missionary colleges came down to what I used to call 'Thirty-Nine Articles with Scripture proofs.' It was not very much more.[14]

We were not, at first, conscious that there was any novelty in all this.[15] Then it began to dawn on us as a very strange thing that the universities and the authorities on the one hand, the clergy and the parishes on the other, did not like our idea of a theological education, nor in the least understand it.

To the universities and the Church authorities education (no doubt a most important matter) was essentially a secular business, intended to give 'broad' interests and views. They knew that 'correct doctrines' are more or less necessary and some knowledge of modern criticism and controversy, but this technical and professional knowledge was a secondary matter.

The clergy and the parishes put a higher value on correct doctrine, and cared less for 'breadth,' but they cared equally little for technical and professional knowledge. All that was really useful could be learnt from a few hand-books, and the parish was its own

[15] *Ad filios.*

54

school. Devoutness, energy, and commonsense were everything. The scornful indifference they expressed for 'Theology' was staggering.

To us theology was not a technical and professional knowledge. We were studying God's view of human life, what God was doing on the Somme, and at Westminster, and at Tilbury Docks. In this our Vision of Theology was part of our Vision of the Church. I do not want to know what you can do with Christ in a church (building) half as much as I want to know what Christ is doing in the street. We were well aware that you must find Christ in the church (chapel) before you will find Him anywhere else (on the football field), but the two are not the same. It is quite possible to find Him in church and never think of looking for Him anywhere else. The worship of the parish church is the key which should unlock the mystery of God in the world. Just so. Is it being used to unlock the mystery? Is it not being very generally used to lock the mystery up, to lock itself up—safely within the church itself?

This 'Kelham theology' of the will of God in the world was a Kelham Gospel to the world. I do not mean that only Kelham believed it. Every orthodox Christian admits that it is in some sense orthodox doctrine, however little he recognizes the consequences. There are no doubt many others who preach it, e.g. (F.R.) Barry. I only say that it was ours to preach, and that we had shaped our whole ideals upon it. We had made it the basis of our education; in that I think we were alone.

We had a certain idea of training in sacrifice,[16] by discipline, poverty, mutual service. We could not expect men to appreciate it unless we were willing to share it with them, but although the life was great fun and very enjoyable, these features were hardly sufficiently attractive to allow of our advertising vacancies in the normal way. As a matter of fact, in the six years at Vassall Road, we never had a tutor who 'belonged' to us. If one left, it was quite uncertain whether we could get another. There could be no better example of the great difficulty of initiating any novel system in a Church so exclusively dominated by individualism. If the

16 *An Idea in the Working,* p. 35.

spirit of self-sacrifice which men were learning was to be maintained, if their self-devotion was to be effectively utilized, it could only be by some system such as is technically called 'Religious.' At least it was quite plain that nothing else could save the house from being the mere freak or whim of an individual.

V

In [1] speaking to you, my more than friends, my sons, of the formation of a religious Society, I am speaking to you of a sacrifice, of
the sacrifice, of man's whole life, embodied, so the Church believes,
in its most perfect form. I will try then first to show you practically
and historically what this form of sacrifice has been to the Church,
what the lack of it has been. Then having grasped the idea as a
whole, we will try secondly to analyse it and understand its principles. Thirdly I may lay before you in some way the forms in
which it seems in this age and in this church possible once more
to make these principles living and inspiring.

You know we have had these two objects: on the one hand to
train men, who might not otherwise have had the opportunity, in
that mental and spiritual discipline, which should make them most
fit for the Divine Service; and on the other hand, the maintenance
of the character, the perfecting of the sacrifice in a way as much
more permanent, as it is deeper. Meanwhile I would beseech you,
my brethren, my fellow-workers in this great cause to pray for me
even while I speak, that I may not mar the fulfilment of God's
Will through my sin, or fail to declare His purpose through
cowardice or self-sufficiency. For who is sufficient for these things
—to declare what the realization of the whole glory of God is in
the life of man by complete surrender to His Will, in an age when
that realization has been forgotten and even accounted a despicable
thing among men. It is not since the Reformation alone that we
have failed to appreciate what is the meaning of self-sacrifice as a
principle dominating the life. That which God gave would not
have been then presumptuously and foolishly swept aside, if the
meaning had not died out from a shell left all too empty, occupied
only, if at all, with abomination. Nevertheless it may be said it was
a presumptuous act, even if the only one which our sins had made
possible: one which the Church mourns and suffers from to-day,
asking in vain for the old traditions and the old enthusiasm, even
at the very moment when men are scoffing at all which makes

[1] Addresses on the Religious Life, Holy Week, 1893.

traditions valuable, or enthusiasm possible. The age is a wise one and asks for the practical and measurable. Of this other spirit it knows nothing unless perhaps of the very measurable cheapness which such a system might produce; but we, brethren, if we have indeed learnt to hold our lives cheap in the Divine Service, I know not why we should only be used to cheapen the sacrifices of others. For the divine glory all that we have, and all that we are, for the convenience of the faint-hearted we need offer nothing at all. And I propose to turn to other days, and see what this principle has been in them and to them, for we shall find that the contraction of spiritual insight has made it difficult not only for others but for ourselves to grasp at once in this present day of what value this principle may be. I shall not attempt to deal with the ideas of any one particular time or group of persons, lest we might think we were dealing with the localisms of an age, not necessarily less contemptible than our own. We want not that which was temporal to the fourth century nor to the second, nor to the twelfth nor to the nineteenth, but that which is eternal to all: and so to ask for those ideas reaching through many centuries, and every part of the Church; not those always which men at the moment recognized as being the most persuasive, but those which we looking at the ages as a whole can see as having the most dominant influence upon them. And here I give God thanks that I am addressing men who have not only sufficient acquaintance with the subject to give a reality to names and dates as I quote them—which, in part only, you can do—but whose minds have been trained to deal with large ideas in that way—not to ask only after the actual event or its consequence, nor after the confessed reason which covered it, but to look for the real influences that impelled or followed. We have seen what the instinctive modern conception is. We will bring it to the test.

The Covenant of God with man is fitted to his double nature of knowledge and will. The former takes cognizance of a definite, invariable principle of order. The will is moved by a variety of considerations. In God's Church of Israel you will find accordingly that while the order of the Covenant centres upon the work of the priest, there is by his side a line of men, at first vague and undefined, yet clearly traceable in course, the lawgiver, then the inspired judge, finally in Samuel settling into manifest shape as the prophet. There seems at times almost an order, there are schools of them, but unlike the priests, it is never by the order as such, but by the individual that their work is performed of reaching the wills of the people.

In the first three centuries of the Christian Church, we find all writers conscious of, some writers wise enough to emphasize that regular ministry of the Church, which just because it is regular and unfailing, as the rising of God's stars, makes the less impression on the mind. You will observe that the regular ministry has gained much since the Jewish days, just because it represents God's covenant in the knowledge of men, and it is knowledge which has gained by revelation. Yet there is need as ever of something which shall represent God to the will, to kindle affections, to inspire, to lift men—not above what the intellect could see to be good, that would be into folly—but rather to energize the intellect itself by opening to it depths of meaning in life, yes and in death too, which that calculating mind of the world, which some call worldly wisdom, can never enter. The fascination with which the Church pondered the life of Ignatius, a life lifted by death out of obscurity into glory, is the first example of this; but when by Divine providence the rescript of Trajan offered to every Christian not mere death, but the choice between death and apostasy, then martyrs became the seed of the Church. Who does not see, looking carefully and weighing accurately just how things are, that while without the episcopacy Christianity could never have continued, but would have dissipated itself merely into one vague philosophy, yet without the martyrs it would never have been at all?

But I want you particularly to observe that on the practical side all this is very different. How many souls must there have been needing the strictest attention lest they should lapse, who did lapse and were lost, because the shepherd was not. How many confusions, schisms, strifes, practical evils were caused by the sudden removal of the best and most earnest men, who can ill be spared at any time, least of all amid so much trial and temptation. Surely the persecutors saw rightly that the removal of the leaders would confuse the body.

The riper wisdom of the nineteenth century patronisingly concedes its languid praise, while it discourages the exultant joy of Ignatius over a life which might have been so much more serviceably prolonged. What blindness! When just half the mounted force of the British army was launched to death through a blunder, England was six hundred cavalry the poorer. She was richer for ever by an immortal memory. In the Scinde war, when eleven men mistaking signals answered with a cheer and charged alone up the hill held by a whole army, and now with the red cord of honour tied by the enemy themselves about their wrists sleep for ever in the Himalayan slopes, the new morning's 'State of the British forces' showed eleven soldiers the fewer for that, but the ranks of the heroes were widened, and nations and churches are strong not by the count of human beings or of effective workers but by the sum of heroism.

With the fourth century the Church entered on other times, on her long peace. Our spirits indeed still answer to the names of Patteson and Hannington, of François Damien de Venster, of those poor boys of Uganda. We still pray for the gift of martyrdom as for a life work, not cut short but accomplished. Yet we cannot but know that this has ceased to be a thing we have at all a *right* to look for. Since the coming of that peace, a peace of this world—not in any special way passing understanding—has possessed the bodies of men. The scene of the conflict is changed: no longer outward it has passed within. The work of the martyrs is in the main done. Yet as before, God has not left Himself without witness to the *wills* of men. If the peace of the world belonged to the body, it was asserting its awful, its horribly fatal right in the soul. There it must be met and there broken. From that peace, men fled as from a plague, where they hardly cared, to the deserts, to the caves, to the icy pillar top, anywhere where they could be so as to contend with this new form of evil. As at the martyrs men scoffed, as Marcus Aurelius, himself a persecutor, called it sheer obstinacy, Tacitus hatred of the human race, so this seemed, and to men to-day seems to have been self-torture and melancholy misanthropy. Again the Church judged more wisely. These men she delighted to call her athletes, her warriors; she recognized in them her martyrs, witnesses indeed. There was in fact a curious analogy between the two. Both were at first irregular. So great a thing was martyrdom that men could hardly see how there could be evil in it. So great a good was self-sacrifice that the Church only slowly learnt that self-will might there lurk. In time she did learn it. Both were first of all to be recognized as vocations. No man would take the state for himself. Good as it was, it was not for all. God who had a right to ask all of all, chose out of consideration for human weakness, not only to ask all only of some, but to make, to others who longed for it, their sacrifice to consist in its renunciation. Again each required regulation, not only lest it should trench upon that other province which was not its own, but also in itself—only, while death is at all times simple if not easy, this careful adjustment belongs especially to the far subtler sacrifice of the soul in life. At first this sacrifice was of the life of the hermit. Presently as the evils and defects of that manifested themselves, this form was discouraged. There were as yet few rules, but some association was plainly necessary, and that association demanded more and more to be considered and arranged.

Now I want you to observe, that just as in the case of the martyrs it was not the opportunity of speaking, nor the attention they attracted which made for God's glory, but death, pure, simple and in itself, because that was the fulfilling of His will; so also in this case it was not for some centuries the convenience of the system for missionary work, or for teaching, or for study, but simply renunciation by itself that influenced the Church—the fact that they at least had according to God's will taken at their right value the glory and the pomp and the pleasures of this world— taken them at their right value and not merely left them but trampled them under foot. To such then is ever calm peace, and to the Church they taught that lesson, while to others was the boundless sea of self-willed action and appetite unrestrained. In time this lesson at least appeared to be learnt. As barbarism gave way to civilization the forms of restraint were recognized as part of the necessity of manliness. They were carried habitually into the business of the world. Yet no more than before could the Church afford to dispense with the life of sacrifice. Self-indulgence was certainly not killed by civilization. It only took a deeper form, which monasticism hardly reached. The Friar was substituted for the monk, to modern ideas a more practical scheme, though why it should be I hardly know. The object of the monk was simply to live as a man ought to live before God, humbly, obediently, prayerfully, finding in God and the contemplation of Him a satisfaction for every faculty. As to it being useless, if the monk had retorted that he had always believed that one's own life was the best sermon, then I hardly know whether through history, about what he actually did effect, or upon the principle of whether this is a good way to teach people, I hardly know, I say, how we can answer him. Certainly we shall hardly be wise as missionaries to assume that the eloquence of the sermons we mean to preach, or the skill of the catechizings we mean to give, will be more to God's glory or have more influence than the holiness and humility which are as much harder to gain as they are less pleasant to exercise.

The friars at any rate of the two great orders sought to present Christ to the intellects and to the wills of men, in universities, or in towns and country-side, wherever people might be reached and souls won. Yet they used essentially that great monastic principle of seclusion, of heart and life; not now of walls. Just as the monk had been shut in that his eye could only look upward; so shut in was the friar by rule and discipline that from above only was his hope; and it was this separation which made his influence. He, a poor and ignorant man, a peasant among peasants, was yet a being from another sphere.

By what causes in the fifteenth and sixteenth centuries all these had alike exhausted themselves I need not inquire. Two courses were taken with them, each with their consequences full of instruction to ourselves. In the Protestant lands they were simply destroyed. In the Roman countries while they were sometimes left, sometimes they too were by one or another (means) destroyed, yet in their place there grew up Societies, freer even than the friars: having their minds more wholly set upon use, employing even holiness, discipline of character, rather as implements for some great achievements than as things valuable in themselves. And because they did so, they also committed in the end great crimes; but however that might be, so potent is that spirit of complete renunciation that before it alone the whole spirit of the Reformation broke in vain. Backed as it was by the freedom of criticism, by the increase of knowledge, by its zeal for harmony with

Scripture, nevertheless while Protestantism dissolved into a chaos of sterile and jangling sects, Jesuit and other missionaries built up vast Christian churches in Africa, in India, in China, in Japan, in South America, captured all the Latin university education of Europe, and that of South Germany. Through their teaching orders, through Oratorians, Rosminians, and countless others, they have so organized their system, taught their people, kept their children, that with an infinitely inferior system to work on, and under, yet they outnumber us in workers, as in devotion, upon every mission field. Like us they had to contend with the unbelief, the immorality, the indifference of the seventeenth century and the eighteenth, with the misfortunes and secularity of the nineteenth, yet by the elasticity and adaptability of associated and disciplined strength, as of many minds following in order one principle or direction, they have come strongly through it all.

Let us turn briefly to our own church. The seventeenth century is the history of a nation which had earned God's curse by robbing Him, of a church which had acquiesced therein. It is a history of long drawn pain. The devotion, the earnestness, the wisdom, which on the part of many marked its commencement, hardly raising any enthusiasm, doing nothing to avert the terrible disaster which fell upon her in the middle, or the terrible deadness which closes round her at the end. Then comes the Church we had earned for ourselves, one indeed practical to the last point, which would know what was the use, if any, not only of the fantastic asceticism which it had cast off, but of all doctrine, of all love to the Divine Service, which having asked the use of everything long ago, found two practical uses left, court influence and a fat living for the priest, morality for the poor—nothing at all for the heathen. This as an alternative even to the wildest fanaticism of the monks of Nitria, or the hermit of the pillar, for the calm peace of the Cistercian, or the severity of the Dominican, or the utter self-abnegation of the Jesuit, hardly seems a satisfactory exchange. Yet I insist it was gained simply as a result of the 'practical' mind.

In this nineteenth century we are wiser still. If we had been in the days of the eighteenth we would not have done their deeds, any more than those of the sixth. We send missionaries, we teach most earnestly at home—at a rate varying for the former from £300–£150 a year and a house, with a wife, for the latter at £150 a year, and a hope of better. With difficulty we have stretched ourselves to the conception of unpaid missionary work for a few years, in Calcutta, in some other missions. I am not anxious to be ungrateful to God for these His mercies. All I ask you to do is, just in your thoughts, in your imagination, to contrast some of those vast societies of which I spoke, with their self-surrender, with their tremendous—to use a military word—manœuvring power, their exact discipline, the unity of their plans, their methods, together with the diversity of their strength, that utter exclusion or separation from even the possibility of personal ambition, with our laxity, self-will, the shortness of time given commonly by a missionary, and to ask yourselves which now comes nearest to the ideal of a Christian sacrifice . . . whether one does not feel oneself in the presence of a force which we do see to be one of the most tremendous reality, and which it seems little short of a matter of life and death to the Church to analyse and, if God will, to use.

The growth of the knowledge of principles is a slow matter. Men, in new movements, do not go by principles, but feeling after what they seek, and avoiding the things they run against, make progress, as if in what to them is dark, but to God light. And only afterwards do they begin to understand wherefore He has done thus with them.

Nevertheless the study of scientific principles has two important works to perform. First, it gives us the means of judging between the essential and the accidental. The man is apt to assume the course by which he himself was led (to be) the only one, to mistake his own strong bias, or likings, for necessities. To the merely practical mind there is no defence against experience. Second, it gives completeness. There is no guarantee that one or any number of experiences have really covered all sides of the question.

Aquinas says: 'The Religious are those who make themselves over to God as a whole burnt-offering.'

We are to contemplate the Religious Life as a form of sacrifice, a self-sacrifice made complete. And the question we are seeking to answer is: 'Is it not possible to have the sacrifice without the

6. *A cartoon of 1909. Fr. Kelly resisting the decision of the bishops to confine ordination to graduates.*

A cartoon by John Perret, 1928

Portrait (1908)

7. *Celebration of Father Kelly's sixtieth birthday, 1920*

"Religion"?' 'Is it, to express the matter more accurately, possible to offer the complete sacrifice of labour without the complete sacrifice of life? Why should we go beyond the threefold necessity of labour without pay, or marriage, or choice?'

Two answers may be given. First, it is to be observed that in any case the very attempt to put the question in an accurate form has shown that it means *incomplete* sacrifice. I do not want it to be understood that the answer is final. To many an *incomplete* sacrifice is the better. I only want to note that this confessedly it is.

Secondly (and this must be longer) I do believe that the practical sacrifice without the spiritual one is very difficult indeed, and can only in rare circumstances and with rare people be made at all satisfactory. I believe that comparatively speaking there are no instances of this thing being successfully accomplished. A work of this kind was indeed accomplished by Selwyn, by Patteson, and a few others, but these were exceptional men, and they themselves admitted how rare and difficult it would be to get others to join them on the same footing. Why should it be rare? It is not so in the Roman Church. The answer to 'why?' is exactly what I think must be sought in theory. This attempt to have a religious life without religion, the sacrifice of work without that of the whole organized self is not new to the Church. There have been married monks, monks in seclusion without vows, and monks in contemplation without seclusion. At the present day an archdeacon has been heard to propose an order in which men should not spend too long over their prayers.[2] What is there wrong in all this? A man cannot really go on living a half life. He cannot live in complete self-sacrifice merely because he thinks it a good thing somebody should. None can stand the temptations of such a state, except by lifting their life as a whole into a new position. We must then understand what this new position is, that we may know how it can be maintained.

Safeguarding his remarks by phrases implying that what He was saying was only of limited application, our Lord's demand for the

---

[2] The reference is probably to F. W. Farrar, whose lectures on *Saintly Workers*, given in S. Margaret's, Westminster, in the Lent of 1878, had a considerable circulation in the 1880s. If so, the tone is not wholly fair, for the Archdeacon, while evidently anxious to avoid shocking his audience, did try to be just to the austerities of monks and hermits.

sacrifice of the whole being took definite shape in two special directions. Upon the one, 'If thou wilt be perfect, sell that thou hast and give to the poor,' is founded the counsel of poverty. Upon the other, 'If a man come to me and hate not his father and mother and wife and children,' is founded the counsel of chastity or celibacy. So far then there is a distinct divine sanction, so understood by the Church and by the Apostles so followed: but again He Himself taught us how we ought most carefully to study not merely to take precept or counsel according to the letter of its statement, but searching into its spirit set our wills upon that. Each of these two sayings is followed by one in which is given to us the limit of that spirit according to which they are to be taken. The words are nearly alike, the sense identical: 'Take up the cross and follow me.' Upon this is founded that counsel of obedience which is the most essentially a following of Christ, who was 'obedient even unto death.'

The Religious Life is ordained to three ends, first simply to forward the spiritual life, second, because it removes certain difficulties in the way of complete usefulness, third, and in the deepest view, to the completeness of holocaust, the whole burnt offering of ourselves to God—while the first two counsels prepare the object, the third counsel, that of obedience, completes and perfects the fulfilment. In the spiritual life three things separate from God, outward things, bodily things, and thirdly, that which is the only temptation in them, the irregular desire or lust for them. Let us ask about usefulness: men are drawn away from the wholehearted pursuit of the divine service, by exterior things, such as money or ease; by domestic objects; above all by personal desires. So finally the divine sacrifice, beginning with the surrender first of outward things, and then of the body itself, is consummated by that of the will.

According therefore to this sacrifice of the will all the others must be taken. Poverty implies to us not merely the absence of a banking balance, but a real surrender of all external cares or regards, a love of poverty as well as its practice. . . . Yet I do not think that an extreme asceticism is a necessary result of this, although it is one result. With the utmost simplicity of life, there may be a cheerful acceptance of all by which we give God thanks, so only that nothing be so loved that it cannot be resigned without murmur or bitterness: and the application of this practically involves a willing community of goods.

The principle of chastity includes more than merely celibacy, which all recognize as one of the first necessities in anything approaching a really completed sacrifice. Just as poverty involves the restraint of all excessive desires for outer things, so this involves the control of all personal emotions. The dislike of a man to be separated from his wife is inconsistent with absolute dedication to the Divine Service. The dislike of a worker to be separated from his bosom friend is very often not less a stumbling-block. But as before I do not see that it need involve our having *no* personal affections at all. I do not find that among the best specimens of the Religious Life, in the age when it was commonest and best understood that any such thing was expected, nor so far as I can see has the attempt not infrequently made to attain so inhuman a condition resulted at all happily. Both as regards the enjoyment of outward things and individual friendship, it is most important that we should clearly grasp the principle and continually strive to realize and perfect in ourselves, a real control of desires and emotions. I do not think extinction need be insisted (upon), but complete discipline must be laboured after.

It is however in regard to the surrender of the will that there is the greatest difficulty. It is precisely this which marks the difference between the real Religious Life, and that form of secular life which some of you will no doubt feel to be rather your vocation, yet which in regard to many, perhaps the larger number of you, I think myself most firmly to be very much the more dangerous. The difference between a secular life such as we have set before ourselves, unmarried, unpaid, without choice of work, and the Religious lies in this, that in the former obedience is given only in regard to work and its requirements, in the latter it is the surrender of the whole will in every particular. I want you to see how because it is the seal and completion, therefore it is its preservation. In warmth it is hard to understand the pressure of cold, and in freshness weariness. To you, young, inexperienced, confident in your own high purposes, with the strength of will fresh in you from long and careful religious discipline, and the fervour of devotion from sacrifice and worship, it may seem hardly possible we should fall. Let your imagination run on to some lonely African village, or Chinese seaport town, the heat and dirt and mosquitoes and ill-cooked food, the sordidness of the heathenism around you, the sneering contemptuous worldliness of the European population, too superior to be atheistic and yet under-rating every sacrifice and deriding every ideal with that subtle mockery which leaves nothing to get hold of. At that moment, will it or will it not be of value to a man to know his fellowship in a Society, which if founded but this Holy Week, 1893, yet is itself but a link to every Christian heroism of a thousand years, which joins him in a bond of similar help to Frumentius and Xavier, to the Franciscans who taught in China where you shall teach, or the Jesuits who laboured and died in Africa where some at least of you shall find your graves, under the simple cross by unknown lakes, in the will of God. If it is not that, what is it which makes these long lines of failures of which little is said, and magazines do not talk, but of which some know. Why do several bishops agree that one of the greatest difficulties in the employment of laymen is that they drift into government employ, because of its high wages; and in the employment of missionary college clergy that they are always wanting to get home to the serene dignity of a married country curacy? Were they men of less aspiration, or hope, than ourselves: or is it not the plain fact that they went to a conflict of which they knew nothing unguarded, unprepared? I do not know whether in the Roman Church such a thing as a secular missionary is known. He must certainly be very rare indeed.

It is necessary to safeguard this explanation of obedience by pointing out that it is to a rule, not primarily to an individual, that a wise obedience is, as far as may be, secured by the fact that the head is appointed by the members, and is removable by them, and that it is a righteous obedience, for no man may be forced beyond his conscience, although of course if the Society through its superior persist the individual must go.

I have dealt therefore with the essence of the Religious Life and tried to show you what it is, that it consists really in the complete sacrifice of will and not merely of work. Now I want to consider two very important questions. First the question of vows. Here there is a consensus of argument which appears to me irresistible. Not only have we got the example of the primitive Church, but I will put one great medieval authority and one modern. Aquinas maintains that it is the essence of Religion to be a state, in which men live, and that to be in a state a man must in some way be *held* in it. Suarez, the great Jesuit authority, says, for obedience there must be a vow—otherwise there is no obedience, there will only be a purpose of following what we are asked. One sees that very clearly in the army. Voluntary obedience is not obedience, nor does it earn the merit thereof; it is mere complacency. Suarez is, I think, absolutely unanswerable. Aquinas wants understanding a little. I do not think I know quite clearly what he means by a state, but in the main the distinction between a 'state,' and the accidental position of an individual is obvious, and of the highest importance. It applies to every particular what Suarez applies to obedience. If by some vow you are not held to your choice, every temptation, every vexation, every pleasure moves the whole question from the beginning. Can you live like that? The will is not really surrendered while it is always studying to return.

It is this that has made me say I would never have anything to do with a scheme which involved temporary engagements. I will be no party to a scheme for going round and asking you every now and then whether you are tired and don't want to have your lives back yet. We want a 'state,' firm, unmoved, content with God's order. Yet as to the form of vow I do not think there need be great rigidity. Aquinas would have recognized as a vow only that which utterly cut off the person from any return unless by a most solemn release by episcopal authority. Vows of that kind neither is the Church ready to admit, nor our experience sufficient to justify. The principle remains however the same. We give our lives to the Divine Service in full and clear intention, praying God to keep us in the mind to which He has brought us. If through our sin or error we wish to retreat, or the Divine Will should cease to direct us, men need no dispensation to withdraw. Thus we are consecrated wholly to our service, yet we are held by no oath which could involve perjury to God.

The life of man is distinguished from that of the beasts in that by which he understands and acts according to reason; thus the life of pleasure belongs to the animal which only feels and moves. The life of man is divided into two corresponding forms, the active and the contemplative. These two to some extent hinder one another, to some extent forward. For it is obvious that while the active life, being concerned about exterior things, necessarily distracts the pure intellect, yet inasmuch as man is a being possessed of a body, he can only attain to the intellectual act by a process or course, in which many outward things take their share.

If the contemplative life cannot exist without the active, certainly the active cannot without the contemplative. The argument by which Aquinas proves that the contemplative life is in itself higher than the active cannot, I think, be met, however much we may be impressed with the opposite and modern opinion, and however much we may feel as he feels that that is the more pre-eminent of which the Church has need. The contemplative life, he says, is in itself the higher, because it concerns what is best in man, i.e. the intellect, and it lasts longer, for it is concerned with the eternal, and it is the likest to God. These our Lord seems to sum up in His promise, 'it shall not be taken away.' This then is its first excellence that it is the final blessedness, when resting from labours we attain rest in the absolute contemplation of the Divine Essence, for there is but one good for man, and that is God, and but one attainment thereof, which is knowledge, as it is written: This is life eternal that they may know. And if still we live on earth, here also is the same perfection for he who would act and labour wisely and to the divine glory must seek God's will, and he who has learnt to know God shall walk thereafter.

It is as abundantly evident by history as it is by philosophy that there must be a body, suited to circumstances, and variable in different times, as well as a spirit or life, i.e. principles which cannot be changed. Both must be kept in mind. The forms without strict attention to the principles will not be religious. The principles, if they are not fitted with suitable forms, will not be a life for long. But besides these vital principles, the principles of the Religious Life in any age or place, there are certain principles of adaptation which I must give.

The first will be that the adaptation must in the main make

itself. We must feel our way, you and I together, with what can be done, as we realize under the pressure of different necessities, to what it is that God is guiding us. I have thought my own way gradually these two years and more. Nine months ago I drafted a first plan. In that short time I have made many and rather sweeping changes in the part of which we have had experience. I have no doubt we shall make many more. Yet I put it out—against the advice of some—because I think you have a right to ask me to show in some kind of way how it can be done.

The second principle is that the form of religious life must be acceptable to a great mass of the religious strength of the day. That I want to insist upon most earnestly, because many people think that the Religious Life can only fit all the very best people of a very exceptional devoutness, and of a very exceptional type of character. That idea will be fatal to us, for we all are—I may without offence speak for others almost as much as for myself—people of the most average spirituality and the most commonplace character. We are glad it should be. I don't think any of us want to be anything else. Poverty, celibacy, discipline are things a very large number of people, ourselves included, have great need of, if they can be secured in a quite simple way. I lay it down as a general principle that Orders requiring very exceptional people are Orders of small influence. I know that is opposed to the common idea. Take the Benedictines for instance: hard as the life seems to us, in an earlier state of manners it seemed very little more than a very plain life. It was accepted easily enough by vast numbers. As times changed, it fell. Where the rule was strict novices could not be got, and obviously where it was laxed it was abused. Now it is reformed, and there are no abuses; but it is felt to be so hard that only people, not merely of very exceptional devoutness, but of a peculiar type of character can have a vocation.[3] How different is the life now with its tremendous and even fantastic efforts after humiliation from the old-fashioned homely monasticism of the tenth century. The result is that while in the eighth (ninth) and tenth centuries they were the very life of the

[3] Here Father Kelly evidently identified the Reformed Benedictines with the Cistercians, neglecting others, and assumed that all Cistercians had adopted the reforms of La Trappe.

Church, the saviours and makers of Western European civilization, now all real power has gone over to the freer communities. What, for instance, has been the influence on France lately of the Cistercians compared to that of the Christian Brothers?

But for that purpose while the life must be sensible and human it must also be thirdly real. Because I do not see that prostration to superiors, degrading penances, and so on—which were not so felt in the ages when they were a reality—are necessary or indeed anything but pedantic silliness, I also do not see why soldierly obedience, real humility, willingness to account oneself least, readiness to be content with the lowest work and place, readiness to be criticized—I do not see why these are not parts of a true Christian character which we shall do well to acquire, and which we shall be very wise to guard and confirm in ourselves by any means we can, seeing how much the world hates them, and how every notion of the time conspires to weaken them.

The fourth is an application of a similar principle. While we recognize, as I think we cannot help doing, the fact that the contemplative life is, taken in itself, the higher, we must admit that the active life is evidently that to which God's will calls us in this age, and with His will we must be content. At the same time we shall not admit with the age, that really life is too busy to allow of prayers being said.

Fifthly, the work that we do must be done in harmony with the diocesan organization of the Church. In times of unregulated temper I believe it really was necessary that monasteries should be much separated off, and as it were individualized. Such times may again arise when our Society may be needed just because it can stand together, and stand separate. I am sure that is not what is wanted now but just the opposite of it.

Sixthly and I think I may say lastly, we shall therefore find the essential work of the religious life in ourselves. If it keeps us in holiness, it keeps us in God's will; and if it keeps us according to God's will you may be quite sure it is making us glorify Him.

. . .

In the first place I have provided a very complete diocesan organization which is to be built up as soon as possible. The Provincial is head of the Society in his diocese. The Director will act through him, and to the Director he reports. My ideal state is that the dioceses should in time all split off and form independent Societies under their own Director, and with their own finance. They might then form their own adaptations of the Constitution, and yet so long as they keep the same principles, and introduce no changes elsewhere which in the opinion of the parent Society are inconsistent therewith, they would keep the same name, and all members passing from one Province to another would transfer their obedience. Thus the parent Society would continue to train for all.

The House Rule is simply the rule of this House. Not only every Province, but every House therein will have its own rule, suited to the necessities of its own work, but of course that rule would have to be accepted by the Provincial. Our rule here is simply the model.

Let us see how this will work abroad. A clause of the Constitution forbids our making any conditions with the bishop as to where our men are to be employed. I think if, as may so happen, we are enabled to pay for the training of our own men, some variation in that might be permitted, yet in the main its spirit should be kept. Our idea is to place in the bishop's hands a number of really trained men who can be relied upon as absolutely subordinate, free from all preferences, equally willing and happy to be appointed to a work if he would like to see whether we can do it, or to be deposed if he thinks that he finds we can't. If however we are, as we certainly shall be, much scattered, what becomes of the brotherhood? That I think is just the point where we need to guard ourselves from some modern follies. If a parochial guild has a rule of saying a daily prayer, and making a monthly communion, so long as that rule is kept the guild goes on and does its work. How many guild parties there are doesn't matter one bit. So we are a Society because we keep a rule, and in spiritual things, and where the superior has a right necessarily to command us, we give obedience. Whether the brother ever sees his superior's or any other brother's face in this life, matters not at all. The use lies here. You have been taught in this house to make a very real devotion and spiritual observance a part of your life. You have learnt how it may in no way hinder but only inspire your work for Christ. You are going among men, good indeed and earnest, but who not having learnt this are confessedly somewhat secular, fonder of running in and out of school and class and farm than—well then of running into chapel. Do you mean to accept their life or to cleave as well as you can to your own? If you accept theirs do you think that ideal of absolute surrender to the bishop or other immediate superior will remain as easy for you as it ought to be—but for others is not? If so, I would ask you, face to face with the temptations, will the fact of belonging to a Society, of being pledged to a rule, of having a superior to whom you are expected to report, be a help or not? I talked a short time ago of those dreary missionary failures. With the acceptance of the secular tone you are of course within reach of that also. I should not be surprised if some of you were indignant at my broadly hinting that some day you may feel tempted to leave the Divine Service for a paid work or for marriage, or in some other—to be quite frank—cowardly and disreputable way. My dear sons, what we certainly have to be afraid of is not this but the growth of secularity of mind, and the diminution of spiritual ideal by which that and every other kind of fall becomes possible.

So far I have dealt with the Society in its most difficult form, when the bishop gives no other recognition than by permitting it to exist. Even so I think you will find the red cord and all that that signifies to you, worth wearing. But we must have patience. God has led us a long way already. As we increase in numbers in your diocese, and in age and experience, as perhaps some are ordained, or others join us who have already entered the priestly office, the bishops will not generally, I think, be unconscious of the usefulness of men who are trained to work together, who understand one another. If some station is given over to our management as a Society, it will be far easier no doubt, for that house will be a centre for all for retreats, for spiritual strength in all ways. You must have patience. It will be for you in years to come by persistence and capacity for self-sacrifice to perform that part of the work, and to find out for yourselves how the rule can be made most useful to you. All I ask you now is, do you feel that it will be of use to you in any case? If so I think God is calling you to His own blessed sacrifice, the sacrifice not of your work only but of your will itself.

I will explain shortly the alternative(s). Where two brothers are, one is superior, and they form technically a 'House,' but in a House of our own where we are permitted to have our own rule, the head is Prior. Besides the brethren there will be others. Some will not be under the rule, considering themselves free—these we may call visitors or residents. If however they accept the rule, but only for a time, not giving themselves to the Society, I call them Associates. Such is your condition at present. When the Associate leaves the House, he ceases to belong to the Society in any way. Men who leave here not as members, leave us altogether. If they join one of our houses abroad, they would become associates again just in the same way as any one else.

Now I must speak about vows. Life vows are useful and desirable, but neither we nor the Church are ready for them. I have said therefore that they may be taken after ten years from joining. On going out the Associate makes a simple declaration that he intends and desires to give his life to the divine service, unpaid, unmarried, and without seeking any other work than what is assigned to him. The member further after a special novitiate of not less than six months makes a similar profession including the dedication of himself in the Society. If the one who had been an Associate desires a paid post, or to get married, or wants to go in for ordination without having been bidden to do so, he can, but he must inform—not the Society with which he has now nothing to do—but the bishop. The latter may require him to leave the diocese because he has left the object for which he was accepted. If a member wishes to be free he must inform the Society, and may be called on to remain three months over and above the time required for a postal reply. In neither case is any dispensation required, because there are no vows.

In regard to private property, the Society of course recognizes no rights. As a matter of convenience and advantage a man is allowed to keep what he may have brought with him unless it is needed for some special reason. In the case of money, the Society banks it, and is entitled to all interest. If he leaves the Society the principal is returned. He must make a will, if there is sufficient money to require it.

In regard to the appointment of officers, the Director is

appointed every five years by a process which will give, I hope, distant provinces a vote in the matter. All other officers are appointed by him, though he may allow, and I suppose generally would allow, election. Two principles I think of great importance:

(1) Every man is bound to accept any work to which he may be appointed, so he is bound to accept any office. He may protest, he may not refuse.

(2) All appointments are made for the furtherance of God's glory, not of man's dignity, and if for some reason a superior thinks he can make a better appointment, there should be no difficulty about it.

And now to God's infinite mercy and love I commend you, as I have done before, asking Him in the path by which you go this night He will be near and help you. Certainly if ever men did need help we do. The closing shadows of evening warn us of something more than a day gone—for a whole lifetime has perhaps closed. A man who has come face to face, not suddenly and by accident, but after careful preparation and deliberately, with a choice of this kind can never be the same man quite again. I do not know whether I seem to you to exaggerate what is at least as far as regards the Church a very simple business. As regards ourselves no doubt we all recognize its tremendous significance. I am sure I hope to God we all do: but we look and rightly not less at the Church. The Church is at this hour surrounded by every kind of enemy, and the traitor within is not lacking. If a man comes to her service and wants to bring with him his own ambitions, his own likings, his own notions of comfort and of what is fitting, to such I say: 'Depart in God's name. Get you gone lest you perish. This is no place for you.' If a man will come for the divine glory alone, let him come, but he will be wise in my opinion if he first carefully disentangle himself from all which gives the world a hold on him, so that he will be ready to do battle without dreading lest in the hour of conflict he may be put to shame. How infinitely difficult it is to free oneself from these ties, especially and above all from one's self-conceit, love of one's own way, love of one's own dignity, you partly know, partly have yet to know. But, dear sons, if you are one with me, you will not care to know before choosing, because you know that however

76

great your weakness the infinite greatness of God is greater still, and our most dear brothers, the Holy Angels, are more numerous than all those that are laid against.

Having now spoken with each in turn and thought over the difficulties and perplexities suggested to me, I want to put this question once more in the simplest way, which I hope none has yet ventured to answer finally to himself, seeing how momentous a question it is, to yourselves of not less, and to the Church of far more, importance than that first decision by which you turned from the pursuits of the world to the Divine Service. For that decision only meant to her one more amid the army of her workers, but in this second she seems to be looking to you for the restoration of that highest form of spiritual life, the loss of which, or the incapacity to restore which, has made her the scorn of her enemies on both sides. And I want you to think of what I shall say, not in the light of your present knowledge or needs, but as by imagination you may, as they will appear to you, when you have had twenty years in the field, and others are sitting where you sit and looking to you to be their examples and sustainers.

What is the difference between the Religious Life and the Secular Life which you offer?
(a) Theologically, God's right over us is the complete surrender of self in goods, body, and will. Out of mercy, His demand is only for the sanctification of them: with in some cases, those who are called to the Divine Service, the sacrifice of our work.

(b) Practically, the true secular gives his work precisely as the clerk gives his. His working hours are differently and more vaguely arranged but apart from work his time is his own, his money also is his own. A clerk may draw low wages or high, or even none at all. His hours may be long or short. But as long as, apart from the claims of the work, he is his own master, it is obvious he is nonetheless a secular. Similarly in mission life, the S.P.G. or C.M.S. missionary with his house, his wife, his comfortable income is palpably a secular. In Community missions the pay is less, yet since the restraint, such as it is, is only imposed for the sake of the work, and not for the sake of the individual, as he is free to use his spare time as he likes, and whatever he has is his own, he is hardly less a secular. The very restriction on marriage exists for the sake of the work.

The difference seems small, but I think you have not found it so in experience. Let me put it dramatically. 'Can I go now?' says a clerk. 'No, I want this letter copied.' 'Vexing,' we say to our-selves, but still the manager has a right to say what the work is, and we are content. But when the Religious superior answers 'No, because it is not good for you,' every fibre in us rebels. We give our work, but who made him master of me. You will recognize this feeling, I think. I am sure I do, and you will see the reality of the difference between sacrifice of self and sacrifice of work.

In this house, our life is Religious. Restraint exists not for your work but because we believe, you as well as I, that you need to learn to be restrained. If when you go to your work you wish to go unrestrained except by your work, go and God be with you. I have not chosen that for myself and I doubt its being good for you, though I believe it would be still worse to force you to a lifelong restraint you could not bear.

If it is a special vocation, who ought to join?
Part of your life will be like that of seculars, part Religious. The essence of the one is work, the Religious superadds the idea of discipline. For all the rest of his life he is a learner, in humility, in obedience, in all spiritual qualities. Apart from experience one would fancy that was good for all, but it is a mistake. Some men are not good pupils. It is hard to say why. It is not, I think, necessarily lack of humility; perhaps their minds are too outward. Even for them it is most important that they should force them-selves for a time into a more disciplined mood, but it is somewhat unnatural. They are often good workers, good teachers: and unconsciously in the process they learn what God has to teach them, but they have not enough power of concentrating their minds upon themselves to learn well of deliberate purpose. All feel the blessing of rule, I think, but to some it is an iron bond which checks what they still want to do. God does not mean you to live in fetters—in His time, you had best go free. Some find the rule

helps and guides them to what they themselves would wish to be. To them I say, keep it as a precious gift of God's. Test yourselves in this. Supposing this house was governed as those abroad will be, perhaps, a good deal by chapter, can you imagine yourself under any circumstances voting for an increase in restriction even upon things you would yourself like to do? If so, you may count the discipline of rule as rooting itself not merely in your habits but in your will. You could yourself be a maker and maintainer of the rule.

The Principles were written about 1892. I drew up the frame of a Constitution in 1893, of about thirty pages in manuscript.[4] I think I had seen the Holy Rule, but it did not seem to fit. I saw the need of keeping Principles, Constitution, House Rule separate. I saw a Dominican Constitution. That also seemed confused, but it gave me an idea of scale. I read Piaget's excellent book on *La Compagnie de Jesus,* from which I got all my ideas—of what to read, and what to avoid. At Coniston, in August 1894, I proceeded to think out, and to visualize, the whole mechanism of a Society of any size (500 if you like), working in three or four continents, and say half a dozen (or a score) of countries, the different grades of people who would compose it, and the relations of different authorities, of the Society and of the Church. To each chapter I prefixed a careful statement of the aim or ideal. I had clearly in mind that one should plan and dig one's ditches before, and not after, the floods came.

The Constitution is my *tour de force,* the highest achievement of which my incapacity was capable. No one could have less experience of how things were done than I had at Southfields, but my mind was fairly ready, and at S. John's, Kennington, one came across people. I knew, to start with, that at colleges, in Religious Orders, and in missions, a good deal went on which had to be smoothed over on the surface of polished Reports, though telltale ripples would appear even there. Rumours circulated, more or less openly; people who had been somewhere dropped hints or told tales of inside difficulties. Some of it might be gossip, scandal, grousing. You can read all that sort of thing in *The New States-*

4 *Autobiography.*

man, and make your own estimate as to the value of the information. Some day you may get to hear more.

Practical people are concerned with actual (i.e. particular) facts. Whether the Tabennesi Sisterhood did do these foolish things, and Lake Tchad mission get involved in some other difficulties, were no concern of mine, unless some day we had to deal with them. I was intimately concerned to know what follies and difficulties were possible, or even can be thought possible, for malicious gossip is also a fact. You can turn to history to see what has happened. Every actual fact dies with its immediate result. Every actual fact—however dead—is significant as an index of the complex forces which brought it about, and which never die. You must understand them, for they are at work on you also.

I tried therefore to picture men's minds as they would be, and the kind of things they might be tempted to do. As the lawyers say in drawing up a deed, even with your best friend, try to make it scamp-proof. The Constitution was a working drawing. Every sentence must be short, formal, precise, and I knew what momentous and wholly unanticipated results might come from a rule that read this way instead of that way. I had to picture what a rule would mean when it was at work.

If I knew little of the Religious Life, I knew a fair amount of constitutional history, of the mind on which its forms were based, and of the effect they had on men's minds. It is needless to say there were some errors, and an odd impossibility or two. Some were corrected easily; some perhaps cannot be corrected now that we are committed to them. Some things I could not anticipate, and left deliberately vague for the Society to make up its mind about. I knew from constitutional history what great changes may come about from a difference in usage and understanding without altering a rule, and I was quite conscious of leaving room for that also. By sheer thinking I had walked into an unknown land, surveyed it and the route there, and I appeal to the Constitution as proof that my thinking is of a quite practical quality. I proceeded to occupy the vacant territory. I did not 'do' anything. Mostly it did itself.

VI

We had had these ideas in our mind for a long time. Reflection added to their strength; clearness could only be gained when we tried to carry them out. At last we laid them before the House in the Holy Week retreat, 1893. There was a short pause, but on May 9th three of us began a novitiate, and by the close of the summer we numbered six. Hitherto we had called ourselves the Korean Missionary Brotherhood, a title somewhat vague and of not very accurate suggestion. We now adopted the name of the Society of the Sacred Mission, by a dedication to the Angels, as our brothers, the messengers of God.

Just before we started one of our men had gone out as a printer to Magila, in the Central African Mission. He found a very strong feeling there in favour of some Community life, which seemed likely to result in a diocesan system. Hearing of what we had done, he urged upon those around him the importance of making their own effort part of a larger whole. Fr. Woodward, priest-in-charge of Magila, opened a correspondence with us, and ultimately it was agreed, with the bishop's consent, that the former should join us on his next furlough, and that a branch should be formed in Magila.

Fr. Woodward arrived in March 1894, and was noviced. We sat down to consider the situation. The necessities of the work required that he should go back very shortly. We had, of course, no experience to guide us, and very little power to deal with. Besides ourselves there were only six novices, but at least we knew what we wanted, and what were the problems we should have to meet. They would be evoked at the moment we began, on a small scale just as much as on a large. We ought to be ready to meet them not with speculative suggestions, but with carefully considered and predetermined answers. Therefore with lavish hands we drew up a complete Constitution. There are many things in our history we may frankly admit to have been mistakes; many which we regret, but which seemed unavoidable; this we have never regretted.

While we were actually getting this far, a movement was preparing in Korea similar to that in Central Africa. There was at

F

least one priest who felt very keenly the need in missionary work of disciplined life under rule. Early in 1895 he came to England accordingly, but adverse circumstances of all kinds hindered any action till September, when he was noviced. He had to return in the following year, and two men who had completed their course were to go out with him.[1]

The Director and Fr. Woodward made their professions on September 29th and October 2nd, 1894. The Constitution was carefully revised and endorsed in Chapter on November 1st, and thence forwarded to the printers. We had throughout acted in accord with our diocesan, the Bishop of Rochester, who gave us warm encouragement; but it was not until July 24th, 1896, after Dr. Talbot, an old and very kind friend of my own, had succeeded to the see, that our Diocesan took the post of Visitor offered to him by the Constitution, and the latter received provisional confirmation.

It was somewhat disappointing to find, as time went on, that the number of serious applications did not increase. In 1895, three men left for Central Africa; and it became necessary to remove three others. Out of an unusually promising list of candidates all but three withdrew in July; and of those, as it happened, one through ill-health had to leave very soon after joining. It seemed clear that there was something still missing.

Hitherto, omitting one very special case, the youngest candidate received was eighteen; but at different times there had been several applications from boys as young as sixteen, and these caused us no small difficulties. At this moment we had several boys who had offered; more than one of whom had been waiting some time. I wrote to them in July to say we would accept them at the beginning of September. It was somewhat disconcerting that, with one exception, all found reasons for declining; but we were now accustomed to new ventures beginning in this way, and felt nonetheless confident that God willed it. As we were all away for our usual holidays in August nothing could be done, even if there had been anything to do. I wrote at once to the one remaining boy to say that we could not take him alone, but that he might

[1] *An Idea in the Working,* pp. 36–8.

count on joining at the end of September. In the first week of that month, within seven days of our return, two more boys had presented themselves and been accepted. Two joined at Michaelmas and two at Christmas.

In the working classes, fourteen is the usual age for apprenticeship. Once when I was referring to this at a clerical meeting, in answer to the usual objection, a certain parish priest added promptly: 'I think our experience is that this is also the wisest thing. Where, as often happens, a boy is allowed a year or two in what is called "a small place" before he settles down, the results are unfortunate.' Every one knows that the vocation to music and to art show themselves very early. Can any parent seriously believe that all these trades or professions are not 'vocations,' that they are not chosen for the child by God's will? Or, are we to believe that this vocation to the consecrated life is the only one which is not given to the young?

In any new life or effort some enthusiasm must be found. It is the wings God gives to help us over the first and hardest steps. There is a very common idea that it is wise at first to repress it, as a test of its sincerity. I confess I once shared this instinct which I now believe to be purely disastrous. It does not follow that that which you can easily put out is not true fire, and kindled by God's Spirit. In this chilly world we might well doubt if so un-Christlike a proceeding could be wise. Young vocations are like young life. Both are terribly easy to kill; but the hardiest men have often grown from a delicate childhood.[2]

I explained the meaning of reality to every candidate in turn. I knew that was more 'pious phraseology.' The house life should be real, anyhow. But it was not. I knew, more or less, that the men were shirking. A really strong man would have knocked them into shape by sheer force of will. I had no force of will. I had nothing to pit against them but an unflinching patience. We would go on till they learnt. Maybe a really strong man would have broken the venture before those feeble roots got a hold in the soil. After six years, with more possible conditions at Mildenhall, things came a bit straight.

[2] *History of a Religious Idea.*

83

I could, no doubt, have done much better if it had not been for timidity, but the most real difficulty was that I had no idea of 'handling' men. I watched men, read them, bided my chance, and, when the time came, I could sometimes get in very effectively. But of the little daily common assistance in small things (what I called planting and hoeing) I was incapable. When I preach I always feel as if I wanted to alter men's whole view of life, there and then (at least in some particular respect). I do not think I ever could go on preaching from Sunday to Sunday, as one ought to do in a parish.

It followed that I had no idea of 'training' men. I could not now give a continuous course of devotional addresses—I might give a course of lectures on the devotional life, but when I have said it, I have said it. I cannot say it again (except to another class) nor could I go on with it. I could not train men; I could not train novices. I do not even know what 'training' really means. I do not think it corresponds to anything of which I have personal experience. I end off very nearly where I began. You see a thing: it constitutes a vision. I do not grasp it: it takes possession of me.

My inability to get on with my own men was serious enough. It was not less serious in regard to the public. Gore started the C.R., I think, a little after us. Mirfield College was about eight years after.[3] Gore was already a noted figure at Oxford, with a considerable following; further, he had an impressive personality, and was readily followed. He had at once, and C.R. has had ever since, a sufficiency of very able workers, and that was of vital importance. S.J. does not stand on Loyola, but on the Decemprimi.[4]

At the beginning of 1897, with a few newcomers, there were thirteen students in the House, which taxed our space very nearly to the uttermost. None of these was likely to go out for several years, while there was an unusually large number waiting to come in, perhaps about ten. This alone demanded something; but further we could not but feel that London was somehow very unsuitable. House room was expensive. It is a noisy and distracting place, and there was no place for recreation. The streets are not enticing. We played a little limp football, but it required half-an-hour's hard walking to reach Brockwell Park.

[3] See *infra*, p. 96.   [4] *Autobiography.*

MILDENHALL

After six years, our work, which had been carried on with the permission of the Bishop of Rochester, now received his formal recognition. Various people encouraged us to go forward. At the suggestion of one who was deeply interested, we began in a small way to form a fund of our own so that we might no longer be dependent on the missions, which indeed were hardly in a position to go on diverting their funds indefinitely. Canon Bullock-Webster, chaplain to the Bishop of Ely, urged our coming to Mildenhall. There was a large Manor House with accommodation for thirty or forty, and beautiful grounds. The Bishop of Ely was willing, the vicar of the parish anxious, that we should.[5]

Mildenhall lies in Suffolk, some twenty miles beyond Cambridge, between Ely and Bury St. Edmund's. It was a beautiful old Manor House of the end of the sixteenth century, with endless corridors, old oak flooring, and other inconvenient joys. There was a garden, the most beautiful that I have ever seen—I dare say it was nothing out of the common, but I am a townsman and new to gardens. It certainly was very beautiful. And there was a little paddock where we could make a small football ground, and we paid for it just what we paid for our two houses in London.

For tutors there were myself and Fr. Drake.[6] There were seven men students and two boy students. We had also four men preparing for lay-work, and an old sailor to cook. During Lent we lay low. Next term, eight new men came, and it was summer. I will not say what particular naughtiness we indulged in. Finally we had a row or two to clear the air, and then—

What happened then was an astonishment. We left London because we wanted room to live and air to breathe. Things had not gone at all as well or as smoothly as we had expected. We hoped they would go better in the country, but we were hardly prepared for the actual result. After our one little bit of skittishness we all settled down and became abnormally good. We did not merely mean to keep rules, we did keep them, with a careful reverence that understood—at least we kept them quite as fault-

[5] *An Idea in the Working*, p. 23.
[6] Fr. Drake was a priest from the Korean mission, at this time a novice. He returned there professed at the end of the year.

lessly as was at all good for our humility. What is far more to the point than any formal observance, now that we all meant the same thing and knew what we meant, there was an end of all suspicion, of all parties. We began to trust one another. We even began to be fond of one another. We ceased to be a College; we became a family.[7]

We were not lost in the wilderness of London, where every one had friends to go and grouse with. We even eased off a bit into a luxurious style of life. We allowed porridge at breakfast three days a week. Ultimately, we allowed it every day. We allowed afternoon tea, and late dinner. This was luxury. It was a long time before we came to allow meat at breakfast. In spite of all, I never thought the men's health was as good as at Vassall Road. Perhaps it was the extra strain of trying to be good, because we did try, and it's hard work if you're not used to it.

We also made games compulsory, and had afternoon lists. A certain Brother Joseph was responsible for that. Above all, we made something like a real lay-brotherhood. In London, there was nothing but study. There was nothing for lay-brothers to do. Now we had a garden, and a kitchen, and a carpenter's shop, and, presently, a printing office.

At Mildenhall, finally, we made a momentous change of system. All through we had one aim. We wanted to serve the Church. The Church needed men, but she needed most a higher devotion, and a devotion which could be used effectively.

We appealed to the enthusiasm of the Church. We did not ask men for the Religious Life, because most people did not even know what it meant. But the three conditions were intelligible: (1) Come and serve God anyway, anywhere; (2) freely and in poverty; (3) without marriage. It seemed to us that if men honestly gave themselves to God in this Spirit, it would be obvious common sense to most of them that they could best serve together as a regiment rather than as free lances. I say 'to most,' for there are always some whom God has made differently, who can only work 'on their own,' who are fretted and restless under a common discipline.

Mildenhall was a very happy place. But though the life was so

[7] *An Idea in the Working,* p. 40.

happy, the results were very unsatisfactory. We were the only place which offered a free training. Men came forward in crowds, as we expected. And they turned back in crowds, often at the last moment. They left in crowds. I believe every holiday someone failed to return. And it was often, especially among candidates, the best men who drew back, while the feebler men came on to drop out later.

The primary difficulty was over vocation. Very many of the clergy insisted that priesthood was a divine vocation, and no superior had a right to turn a man off to gardening. This extraordinary idea of vocation gave us incredible trouble. On that point we would not give way, but any system must be intelligible in itself, so that the authorities may work consistently. It must be intelligible and reasonable to men in the House, who have to live under it. It must, in the end, be intelligible to those outside, who may in time want to enter it. Our system was not understood outside. We hoped people would come to understand us, but we began to realize that the three conditions on which it was based had ceased to have any real meaning.

We would not promise ordination. But in fact men came either with a definite offer of lay service, or in the *hope* of ordination. And, although we said nothing, it was plain enough to us and to the man, what we were going to do. Furthermore, we had very little choice. At first missionaries encouraged us in believing that there was an almost indefinite opening for lay workers. It is not so. S.S.M. can use all kinds of people, the secular missions, only in the rarest way. It was clear that lay work was not a genuine alternative. So also 'no pay' was simple enough when we had only Korea and U.M.C.A. It was absurd if we were to send men to English parishes. The question of marriage is the most important of all three. But it was little use expecting a mere future ideal to act as a present 'condition.'

The aim for which the system existed remained the same, but it was no longer possible to reach those ideals in the old way. We trusted to the spirit of the House. It must teach its own principles. We would take men for ordination but we chose them on the ground that the Church had a right to select those she wanted because they were the best available. If later on they did not prove to be the best, they must go. They came for her sake, not their own. Instead of the 'intention' of poverty, we accepted the principle of repayment (already adopted at Mirfield).[8] We expected a rapid growth. If the men who went through repaid the bare cost our money would pay for staff, and failures.

Once the ordination question was put in a shape that the outside world could understand, we began to grow by leaps and bounds. Mildenhall would no longer do.[9]

The outside limit of accommodation was only fifty, and at the beginning of 1901 we were nearly forty. The remaining space would not keep us much longer; as a matter of fact, the limit was passed in 1903. Further, our original lease was only for seven years, and our landlord was anxious to resume possession. We started, therefore, to make plans. In January 1903 we found Kelham. It had every quality but one of those we required. It was accessible, on the Great Northern main line, with a Midland communication to the West. It was near a town and yet well out of it, with good grounds, with bathing, with ample accommodation for a hundred men, with town water, at a rent even absurdly within our means. We need not here expatiate on the splendours of its Gilbert Scott architecture—the carved stone and vaulted ceilings, the lavish marble, the plate glass windows, and the great marble staircase which is not there, for the house was never quite finished. That is a disappointment. We struggled against it, but we feel we *ought* to have a marble staircase. In the end we filled the space up with rooms. We could wish also that the house was a little higher up. It is not bracing, but the rooms are very airy, and, after all, it might be much worse. It is on gravel. After wearisome legal formalities, we were allowed to lease it for a term of seven years, subsequently extended to fourteen, and in July 1903 the move to Kelham took place.[10]

Every one now knows Kelham, but it was a very long battle before we could win a recognized position. Remember again what our aims were. We were not thinking of ourselves at all. We had

8 See *infra*, p. 96.
9 *Ad filios.*
10 *An Idea in the Working*, pp. 65-7.

no aim even for the Society as such. We were thinking of the Church. The Church needed men, in numbers, but still more in devotion, and hardly less, in training. We conceived of those in the simplest way. The Society was a means by which devotion could be made more real, permanent, and effective to the glory of God. It was only very slowly that we learned how very complex and difficult these things were. In the abstract every one accepts them as obviously desirable. When you come to the point, as it is difficult to be really devoted or really 'educated,' it is extraordinarily difficult to get people to see that they mean anything in particular.

If we could make a strong body of *organized* devotion, we might hope to keep the ideal in being, and the Associates who went out from us as secular clergy might, and we hoped would, make possible to the Church the ideal of a priesthood which could live among working men as working men themselves live. The Kelham life need not be an ideal which men once went through at College; it might be a normal type of living. If the S.S.M. was weak, the few men we sent out for ordination would be just absorbed by the prevalent system.

The examining chaplains said with joy—'These men have learnt to think,' so after all Kelham had done something for them. They make quite good curates, but there is nothing, so far as I know, to distinguish them from any good Catholic curates. To modify the chaplain's words, I should say: 'These men have all by now forgotten how to think.'

Of the Society part, I will not say much, but all this opposition and strife had a disastrous effect even on those who did join. They at least must see the Vision, but it is difficult to see Visions in a blizzard. There was also a great difficulty over ordination. We could not send everybody to Africa. We could not take up new ventures with young deacons. Curacies were inevitable, and they offered a chance of outside experience. The curacies were fatal. The universities were still more fatal.

The work of the Church rests in the end on the common priest, ministering to common souls. The work of the parishes is practically everything. When I criticize parochialism, I am not going back on that. I am talking of 'parochialism' as we have it. I have

89

spoken of the curious idea of middle-class respectability which it
has absorbed, of its consequent lack of 'devotion,' and of the
narrowness of its theological outlook. We saw these defects more
or less dimly at the start; we only learnt their significance more or
less clearly as we went on.

The Church of England has in fact chopped up the whole of her
work into what are fundamentally one-man jobs or 'spheres,' by
drawing a line along four streets on the town map. The area thus
bounded is called a parish, and has a vicar. The vicar is virtually
free to run this area in his own way, according to his own ideas.
He calls it 'my parish' and 'my work.' There is just himself to
look to. It has the extraordinary joy of self-fulfilment, such as an
artist takes in his painting, or a musician in his music. In fact
many people cannot do it. But then to realize your own incom-
petence is not only very difficult, it is a most dangerous spiritual
act, for to admit failure is almost inevitably to acquiesce in failure.

This isolated individualism has produced in many of the clergy
an extraordinarily mental nervousness. I have known men whose
theological interest was confined to what would go into a sermon,
who if you talk of any question affecting the Church at once reply :
'Ah yes. I am constantly telling my people.' Missions only bring
up missionary meetings. Nothing interests except what can be
translated directly into parochial terms. But the most disastrous
effect is theological. Practically they are not even interested in their
parishes, but only in what goes on, or may go on, in the four
walls of the Church, and the Parish Room. Football clubs are a
means of 'keeping the young men together.' You ought to be
interested in the discussions of your working men, because then
they will be interested in what you have to say, and 'come to
Church.' It all ends in that. It does not occur to them to be
interested in labour questions because God is.

The clergy are so absorbed in getting people to 'come to Church'
that the Church services have become a substitute for God. To the
clergy (generally) the mass does not lead to the street, because
they are wholly preoccupied in getting the street to come to Mass.
If the Church is to be identified with the sum of parochial spheres
of work, then the Gospel must be identified with religion and
devotions.[11]

[11] *Ad filios.*

Catholicism offers the plain man an observance, which is at least within their reach, and which has availed to save thousands from that moralist Pelagianism which I take to be the most godless of all heresies. It has been the alliance of sacramental faith with evangelical piety which has made the later forms of the Catholic movement into the most effective religious power to-day, and yet Catholicism based its rules of observance on the authority and immemorial teaching of the Church. This conception of intellectual submission involves an ideal of a beautiful humility, but it is not an ideal, not a form of humility, which is possible to many men, especially those who have been trained in scientific schools. We are bound therefore to sympathize with the aims of the *Lux Mundi* school, even if one feels that it is too evidently in the nature of a compromise to affect the situation very deeply. It well recognizes that there are two elements which want recognizing, and those who are not inclined to think very deeply or have given it up in despair may be content. Few genuine thinkers however are likely to be satisfied with unresolved antinomies, or with balance for its own sake.

This then is the explanation of our present position. It is that vast mass of people who are not constitutionally capable of piety or of submission to authority, as these are commonly understood, who have fallen back upon a Pelagian and anti-dogmatic morality.

The real and central hinge of all hope of a religious regeneration, lies in substituting faith as the dominant religious motive instead of feeling; and, for its object, the actual power of God in the place of 'piety'; the delight of learning, beholding, obeying, in the presence of all the width of its operation, for the mere enjoyment and possession of a comfortable sentiment within one's own individuality. The first is possible to all men, most to the busiest, for it is the guide, the motive, and purpose in what they have to do. The second is a thing apart, belonging to a world of its own, accessible to the leisured.

While then it has been the whole substance of our aim in teaching to show how religion can be brought, through knowledge of the will of God, into effective possession of men's whole lives, all existent clerical training has regarded theology as a technical study, only to be pursued as a voluntary and scarcely necessary addition after the serious business of education was over, just because it was based on the latter ideal of religion. The result is manifest in all schools alike. The evangelical idea was developed without any philosophic basis, and to this day the growth of any keen intellectual life is always fatal to its hold on the mind. The catholic study of theology, though real and effective, has been too much cramped by exclusive attention to authority, in the sense of precedent. Philosophy therefore has been left to the latitudinarians who are more anxious to pare Christianity to what they think it ought to be than to learn what it is.

We have therefore suffered somewhat from the suspicions of all schools. The evangelical feels that we are reaching into an atmosphere where he cannot breathe; to the catholic we seem to be abandoning what he takes to be the only safe ground; the latitudinarian resents an invasion of his ground in the name of a faith he thought he had superseded. So far as we ourselves are concerned these objections may not be felt very seriously, but so far as the adoption of our method is concerned, they reveal what is our greatest difficulty—no one knows what we mean by theology.

So far what I would maintain is (1) that the religious reformation for which we are all hoping must, like all real and permanent religious movements, be founded upon a new theological principle : (2) that this principle must be constructive. Men receive life from the beliefs they gain, not from those they have lost, and in the new state they must seek 'not to be unclothed, but to be clothed upon.' (3) Neither is the principle to be 'a new thing vainly invented,' but new only in the sense in which the teaching or thoughts or ideas of Cyprian, Origen, Augustine, Athanasius or Cyril were new, in which life is always new, growing from the latent seed of the one Sower, having waited for the spring.

If this be sound, we have so far justified our immediate method, the work of the S.S.M. College, and its second main principle of making theology the basis of clerical education. The incapacity of Englishmen to follow principles or theories of any kind makes them suspicious of theology in any shape, and therefore, not only unwilling to criticize the ground of their action, but also extremely ready to assume motives in us in place of those which they fail to understand. I do not think we have any reason to be astonished

at this; there is ample reason to wonder rather at the rapidly
growing sense that an education of this kind is right. The
theological movement however is an entirely different matter.
I would not say that it lies altogether beyond the possi-
bilities of an individual. Wesley is a proof to the contrary. The
Oxford Movement was effected by at least a group of individuals.
Westcott and Gore have exercised a tremendous personal influence.
But we must observe, first, that all these were men who did
possess a marked and exceptional personal power and, secondly,
that the work of those within our own time has only resulted in
the formation of 'schools of thought,' not in anything national,
not in anything we might call a regeneration. The conditions of
our time seem to be unfavourable to personal influences. We are
all too eagerly sceptical and 'independent' to follow any one; too
anxious about opinions to be deeply swayed by a teaching.

Men ask, Why cannot we do again by Wesley's methods what
Wesley did?—and others, Why cannot we do again by Newman's
methods what Newman did? I answer, nothing is ever done *again*.
I ask, is it not possible that something like what Wesley effected
by sermons, and Newman by writing, might be done by the, as
yet in the Church of England, new and untried forces of organization? There is at least one good reason for hoping as much. Where
the strength of feeling has dissipated itself in emotionalism and
the strength of teaching in the jangle of opinions, there all the
more the manifestation of power reveals actuality; and that manifestation is organization.

Now herein is the wonder, not to ourselves perhaps, but certainly
to others. Kelham is to them a very real power; from their way of
thinking they assume it must be an individual power. But while I
am (as its head) a conspicuous person, they are all as conscious as
any of us that my own personal influence, whether as a writer,
as a thinker, or as a man, outside our own circle, are just exactly
nil. In talking to men without, I can feel the growing sense of
bewilderment, the sense of a power they do not understand, but
which I know, and which we know, to be the power of an
organization, of a band of men who, not by virtue of opinions,
but in the clear simple conviction of what God has given them to
know, work steadily in one unity for one purpose.[12]

[12] *Ad fratres* (1906).

All modern religion is based on the principle of individualism, and I assert that this is as true of Catholicism as of Protestantism. The demands are different, but the ends are the same. Both agree in the use of the phrase, 'the preciousness of the single soul,' and in the duty of moving heaven and earth to make one convert. That the single soul is precious in God's sight we have express warrant of Scripture for believing, but we have no less warrant for affirming that no single soul is in a state of salvation so long as it is precious in its own sight. Salvation is in Scripture only a salvation of individuals so far as it is a salvation from individualism. There are in the end two things for which a man may live—God and himself. The deplorable thing is that while all religiously minded people recognize that humane 'culture' may be only the gilding of that idol of self which remains essentially detestable, they find it much harder to recognize that just the same thing is true of religious culture. Is there an expression of the fundamental basis of religion more false than Newman's saying 'God and his own soul'? True religion is forgetfulness of self, faith in God's will, purpose in its acceptance, joy in His operations, in the manifestation of His glory. Its practices are only efforts, exercises, to call the mind back to this central purpose, but its substance is nothing more than to rejoice in God.

I do not want even to seem to criticize religious societies such as Cowley. God has called them and given them their own work. They have done it far better and more successfully than we have ours; but it must be plain that for this which we set before us, this of which we are to be witnesses, a system of perfected devotion, a system involving some specific separation from the normal life of the Church is no use at all. We cannot be ascetic. The Son of Man came eating and drinking, and to appreciate, to enjoy, the reasonable pleasures which God gives, are really part of our work and witness. Again, we cannot have a separate life. We are bound to find God's will where He operates. We cannot seek a separate and distinct work. It is men, it is the Church as made for men, which is our special sphere of usefulness. It is really part of our calling that we should enjoy food, sights, games, that we should be tremendously interested in politics, business; that we should seek the commonest and simplest forms of Church work.

BEANS

Asceticism, devotion, separation, are all good, for they are witnesses by men of rich spiritual gifts that sensual pleasure and worldly occupation are not things in themselves good, cannot dominate a true human soul. We are only witnesses that all things are good, if God is seen in all. We, being just the commonest possible sort of men, are witnesses to just the commonest and simplest things. Yet we too are separate; we too have our own calling. All true hearts make sacrifice to God. Some have given up enjoyment; some have given up their way of life, some their work. We are too small for great things, but we have been called to give ourselves. Our rule exists but to ensure in us the reality of this one thing. Our life is very plain, but when we get our Sunday breakfast, we make no shame to enjoy it and laugh. When we come to a fast day, there are beans, and we enjoy the contrast and laugh again. In games and holidays, we enjoy ourselves and give thanks to God, and when we come under discipline once more we enjoy our own helplessness and submission and laugh also. They are not personal pleasures; we laugh with the joy of seeing God's will fulfilled in the knowledge that it is always good.

I am a soldier, and I speak as a soldier. In two ways an army may be lost; if it breaks up, or if it takes refuge in a fortress. Big or little, advancing, standing fast, it is always a power to be reckoned with so long as it holds stubbornly together and keeps the power of moving in the open field. The Prussians, beaten at Jena, broke up to make a disgraceful peace. The Austrians at Ulm fell back on their fortifications—to lay down their arms. In 1813 the allies beaten at Bautzen and Lutzen would neither break up nor seek their own safety, and shortly after they destroyed the Napoleonic empire at Leipzig. But if my military lessons do not commend themselves, then I speak as a priest after the fashion of a priest:

In the way of Thy judgments, O Lord
have we waited for Thee,
Therefore have I set my face as a flint
and I know that I shall not be ashamed.[13]

13 *Ad fratres* (1906).

Kelham and Mirfield

The Community of the Resurrection was planned by a group of friends at the Pusey House in Oxford in the summer vacation of 1889, and the rule tested by four of them that autumn, but no professions were made until July 25th, 1892. The planning of S.S.M. began at about the same time, but did not reach the stage of possibility until May 1890, or of experiment until January 1st, 1891. The name was first used, according to the contemporary Journal, at the Michaelmas festival, September 29th, 1892. The first novices were admitted on May 9th, 1893, and Father Kelly made his profession at Michaelmas, 1894. On this account C.R. began earlier. On the other hand it may well be said that it did not take its permanent shape until after Frere succeeded Gore as superior at the beginning of 1902. The theological college at Mirfield was planned before this, but opened afterwards. According to G. L. Prestige (Life of Charles Gore, 1935, p. 218) the idea of this arose out of a visit to Fr. Kelly at Mildenhall by Fr. Paul Bull (May 29th, 1901). It was in the summer of 1902, according to the Annual Report, that the S.S.M. 'decided on dropping the old conditions of acceptance, and substituting a simple basis of repayment of actual cost of residence after ordination.' [14] When it is said (p. 88) that this had been 'already adopted at Mirfield,' this must refer to a prospectus, for the college did not yet exist. The Community had been at Mirfield since 1898, 'about eight years after' the beginnings at Vassall Road. This must be the reference on p. 84.

The College after 1902

The change in the conditions of acceptance in 1902 is more important in retrospect than it appeared to be at the time, and probably in 1921 (the date of Ad filios). The 'three conditions' were unrealistic from the start to this extent, that some of the most serious applicants were the most reluctant to profess an intention of living without pay or marriage as a condition of acceptance before they began their training. In practice those who did not join the Society (and it was never expected that all would join) found it increasingly difficult to fulfil them, since the missions had little use for theologically-minded laymen, not specially trained for particular duties. Those who wanted priests trained with the S.S.M. generally wished them to serve a curacy first in an English parish. Curacies made 'no pay' obviously unsuitable as a condition of acceptance, and in the idea behind the three conditions 'no pay' and 'no marriage' were interlocked.

[14] Abandoned only after the Second World War.

96

The really important difference is that from 1902 students were accepted whose primary intention was to offer themselves to the Divine Service in the ordained ministry. They were trained under conditions of selection and testing elsewhere unknown, with an idea of vocation set before them that was very different from the normal type of English clerical life. But no pledge was exacted from them except a promise to repay the cost of their training, and, at first, to refrain from marriage until this was done. In practice these new conditions proved as unrealistic as the old, for rather different reasons. Some who went to the mission field were rightly and reasonably excused. Others found it harder than they expected to save something like three hundred pounds from a curate's pay in a time of rising prices. The sense of financial indebtedness to the Society remained, and cast a shadow over the lives of some of the most responsible students while they were still in the House. To them the conflict between the sacrificial idea of the priestly life and the standards of clerical duty normally accepted in the Church of England was a very real one, to which they must each find his own solution.

This tension has been eased since the Second World War, first of all by the general acceptance in the Church of England of the principle that candidates for ordination to the ministry should be selected, tested, and trained thoroughly, and that the cost of their training, whenever necessary, should be borne by the Church in some way. Another factor has been the change in the secular position of the clergy. Curates indeed are far better paid than they were, but no one any longer imagines that incumbents are well off in relation to the higher standard of living of society in general. To many the sacrificial approach to the priestly life commends itself by its realism. They come to be trained under religious discipline for a life that will be, in any case, a bare and hard one, whether they find a vocation to the Religious Life or to the mission field, or serve in a parish at home. If this way of training does not suit them, other ways are open. The central authorities responsible for the co-ordination of methods of selection and training for the ministry of the Church of England have not adopted the Kelham system or any other, nor is this likely, but they have been influenced by it, especially in methods of selection, and they do take it seriously.

G

VII

According to the Constitution of the S.S.M. the Director is elected by the Great Chapter, itself elected every ten years by Provincial Chapters, who are represented in proportion to their size, but at the General Chapter, a like body which normally meets five years after (but may in emergency be summoned earlier or later), he offers his resignation. At the next Great Chapter, he resigns. The Constitution, while leaving the way quite clear to the election of a Director to a further term of office, by no means takes his re-election for granted. Fr. Kelly had been so re-elected in 1905, but by 1910 he had been in charge for twenty years, and it was only to be expected that the possibility of a change in leadership should be seriously considered.

The growth of the Society had not kept pace with the increase in the number of students at Kelham, but it was still sufficiently rapid to raise problems of administration. Nearly all the professed were young. One priest of some experience, Fr. David Jenks, who had been on the Archbishop's mission to the Assyrian Christians, Fr. Alfred (Fr. Kelly's brother), one other young priest, and one graduate from Dublin already prepared for ordination, had come to join the Society at Mildenhall, but only one man with academic qualifications had joined the Society at Kelham before 1910. Otherwise all the brethren had begun their higher education at Kennington, Mildenhall or Kelham, although two had since graduated at Oxford and Cambridge.[1]

The Society's original connection with Korea had ceased, but commitments in Africa continued, and since 1902 had been extended by the acceptance of responsibility for the work of a dwindling missionary brotherhood, the Society of S. Augustine at Modderpoort, on the border between Basutoland and the Orange Free State, with missions in both. South Africa provided a field for young and active men, but they required older leaders; Fr. Alfred and Fr. Drake (returned from Korea), were sent with them. One other priest with academic attainments followed for reasons of health. The only way of recruiting tutors for the house at Kelham was to send the abler students among the

---

[1] This may be the place to correct a mistake unfortunately given wide currency in Canon Roger Lloyd's sympathetic and generally accurate account of the aims of the Society in *The Church of England in the Twentieth Century*, Volume I, 1946, pp. 187–97. Kelham never decided 'to refuse to take university graduates' (p. 194). Only a few came, but these were and are welcome. From such men two of the five Directors of the Society since Father Kelly have been chosen, while another was for many years Subprior at Kelham.

professed to the universities. The rest who could not at present be employed in existing works, were serving in parishes. Under such conditions, as we have seen in the last extract from Ad filios, *stability and discipline were hard to maintain.*

Fr. Kelly himself was continually conscious of the need for some senior recruits, if the work of the younger men was to be efficiently organized, in order that the Society might make an impact on the Church as a corporate body, and not be overshadowed by his own singular personality. He probably also believed, not only that Fr. Jenks inspired more confidence in the house, but that he could more easily command attention from those without. At this time the problem of qualifications for candidates for ordination was attracting more and more attention, and the bishops of the province of Canterbury had committed themselves to the view that after 1917 no one should be ordained without a degree, and a year's further theological study after this. In one thing Fr. Kelly was plainly wrong. The obstacle to the recruitment of older priests, trained elsewhere, into S.S.M., had nothing to do with him, but rather arose from the whole situation of a priest coming to Kelham into a novitiate of young men, generally from a class other than his own, who in their own belief, and probably in his, were already being educated in a theological discipline which he himself had unfortunately missed. By contrast, if he went to Mirfield, where the Community did not then seek recruits among their own students, he found a group of priests trained in different places, with different backgrounds, in most cases like his. If the problem now is rather different, this is because the whole standard of theological education in the Church of England has been raised, so that despite the continued difference between theology at Kelham and theology in the universities, it is easier for those trained in one discipline to understand the other.

In 1910 the General Chapter was divided on the question of the acceptance of the Director's resignation. Kelham, and the clergy in England, were in favour, the Provinces in Central and South Africa against. These Provinces were represented partly by delegates working in England, who are more strictly bound by their instructions than representatives. The South African instructions were strict, but Central Africa allowed some latitude. The votes were precisely equal, a contingency which the framers of the Constitution had not foreseen. A deadlock resulted, which could only be resolved by the initiative of the Director himself. This is the background of the following extracts.

Every one knows what education is and how it is done. Especially everybody knows what theological education is. Everybody knows what the Religious Life is, and everybody knows what Catholicism is. Everybody hates ideas, and being asked to listen to them. Ideas are worrying enough in themselves, but people will put up with them from a man of known ability, such as Gore. He belonged to a very important group, all of whom were scholars, fellows, and some were professors. He wrote books and every one bought them.

Nobody could deny that the College went on, and produced results. H.K. (Fr. Kelly) became an eminent person, but no one could see why he should be. I had nothing to show, and no influence. I wanted to write books, and did write a few. Some of them sold moderately, some not at all. None of them produced any real effect. [B.W.] Randolph [the Principal] of Ely said to me early in 1910: 'The difficulty to me is that S.S.M. is just you.'

I do not know exactly what Randolph meant; I doubt if he quite knew himself. Did he think that I liked running things alone? There are people who do. To me it was impossible. Did Randolph mean that our system was too much off the conventional line to win outside confidence, so that it was not really comprehensible to anybody except myself? I think that is unquestionably true. There were a good many ideas. Were they so hard to understand? Did Randolph mean only that I was personally not a man to inspire confidence? I think he rather liked me, and would not have said it, but it is true all the same.

Someone else however believes that H.K. is a profound thinker, but the most obscure, difficult, even muddle-headed writer (and speaker?) known among men. I expect that also is true, partly because of the infinity of labour which it takes me to get anything said at all. Some people can write what they want straight away. It often takes me days to get started. Even then, I have to keep writing and rewriting before I can get a tolerable statement. And simplicity is the one thing I strive after endlessly. I am always asking people to tell me which are the obscurities. If a man thinks you are obscure, he is evidence, jury, judge, and executioner. By being accused, you are proved guilty of not being plain to him. But I am still perplexed over it. A number of quite untaught folk have appraised the simplicity of what capable people called unintelligible. When I lamented my incapacity to Neville [Talbot], he said: 'Not a bit. You are as plain as can be, but we are all looking the other way and don't like it.'

I admit I have always had two fancies in my head, which were perhaps impracticable: one that ideas could be made comprehensible, and that people when they had got to see them might be got to follow them; the other that anybody, more or less, could be taught to understand anything, and might in that way learn to do things fairly well, provided that he would take pains and go on at it, and further, that he was taken by sufficiently easy steps. In spite of my own failures I am not sure that I do not hold these strange beliefs to-day, at least as regards most people. Their unwillingness to take pains is what puzzles me.

Dealing with priests was a very different and, for me, a difficult matter. They were grown men, younger than I was perhaps, but then, truth to tell, I was never anything more than a boy playing at being grown up (I became a man, rather suddenly, after 1910, at the age of fifty). They were all much abler than I was, better scholars, and for all real purposes, more experienced. They had formed minds, and much stronger characters. Our ideal of education and our moral conception of the House were acceptable to every one, but both these, and our ideal of dedicated service (how I have wished I had called it 'The Society of the Divine Service'— I missed a turning there) rested on a certain theological conception, which to me was the life of the whole; to men who had already 'done theology' at a university, it did not come at all easily. Some of our priests were perplexed, but presently learnt to understand, not without making difficulties. There were others to whom doctrines were everything, and my 'faith' was foolishness. They made no effort, and little pretence, to understand or 'enter into the cloud.'

At Kelham the shadow came nearer, and took a shape more grim. I knew things were not going right. In 1909 the Home Province had made up its mind to a new election. After a month or two there was a hitch. The Home Province knew me well enough to want a chance for a fresh start. The Provinces abroad would not agree. I saw a really glorious chance. And we came to Chapter. The difficulty came up. It was known I had a solution, and I was sent for. I read a statement [2]:

[2] *Autobiography.*

As required by the Constitution I have as Director placed my resignation in the hands of the Chapter. During both the preliminary discussions, as well as during the sessions of this Chapter, it seemed to me an obvious duty that no expression of my own opinion on the subject should be made known. I could not give one unless it was asked, and I have been in entire agreement with the Chapter in thinking that it should not be asked. The Society must act for itself.

The circumstances are now somewhat changed. I have known for some time past what was likely to occur, and I have been considering very carefully what I ought to say or do. On the one hand, it is an act of great presumption for a single individual member of the Society, whoever he may be, to set up his own opinion. If the Society had agreed with anything like unanimity on the course which ought to be followed, I think it would have been. I believe I am right in saying that this is not the case.

My own action then is determined by these considerations:

(1) I believe the Society is at the present moment in a most critical position. A right decision will send her forward full of enthusiasm and power. A wrong one may involve the greatest disasters.

(2) If the Society is not merely to make a right decision, but to profit by it, it must both be right, and be accepted. It must be accepted by the enthusiasm of every one.

(3) My position as Director has of course given me special opportunities of forming an estimate of what the Society requires. In general, the Director ought not to take any part in the matter, but I believe I see my way to a course, if the Chapter will assent to it, by which a unanimous agreement of the whole Society can be reached.

(4) Whether even this would justify the Director's intervention, I am not prepared to say, but I am conscious that the difficulty has largely arisen through the peculiarity of my own position as first Director of the Society.

I feel it no more than my plain duty to lay before this Chapter my conviction that possibly even the continued existence of the Society, certainly her whole chance of making any effective progress in the fulfilment of her calling, depends first of all on her electing a new Director at once, or as nearly at once as the forms allow.

I have not formed this conviction hastily. It rests on four deliberately formed judgments:

(i) That I have my uses and capabilities, but that my work as Director is done, and that while the lines of principles may remain, on the practical side it is now a failure. And I am prepared to show that both the Church, and all the members of the Society— although many will deny it, and have voted against it—fully share my convictions.

(ii) That I am in consequence wholly out of place.

(iii) That the present condition of the Society imperatively calls for a new departure.

(iv) That anything I can do, I can do better without being Director.

To have ideas, to be able to explain them to students, is the business of a teacher. I am exceedingly anxious to believe that I have been a great success, at least as regards my own children, though unfortunately I could never persuade the British public of that interesting fact. But the one business of the Director is leadership, that is to get men to carry ideas out, and here I have wholly failed.

Let us begin with the Church. I have succeeded in persuading a number of bishops, and a good many other people that Kelham College has a remarkable system for training men. I have per-suaded—probably—most of the bishops that S.S.M. was an honest and well-meaning Society. But I have never yet persuaded the Church or any practical body of people to accept or to consider even the college as a serious system,[3] or more than a freak of my own.

It is much more serious that I have never for the last two years persuaded any one that the Society had any serious existence at all. Clergy in reasonable numbers have gone to Cowley; clergy of the highest ability have flocked to Mirfield. It is years and years since any one gave a serious thought to us. My work is done, long past done. I had plans, I have mapped them out and explained them.

[3] This clearly refers to the threat to refuse ordination to all non-graduates, including those trained at Kelham (*supra*, p. 99 and plate 6).

Every one has heard everything I have to say and is tired of it. They are Kelly theories, or the Kelly theory. They are very interesting and Fr. Kelly is a remarkable man. My abilities and shortcomings were excellently summed up by a certain member of a committee on which I had urged a certain policy. Of course the committee did not accept it; but the archdeacon said, 'Fr. Kelly's speech was extremely interesting. It has made me think.' I consider this an achievement on my part of which few men are capable, but there it is. I can make people think; I cannot get them to do anything.

The obvious conclusion is that I am in the wrong place. I am a staff college lecturer, but not a commander. I may be an organizer, but what you want is a leader. A staff college lecturer is at a disadvantage in the field. The lecture manner is unconvincing in war, and his own pupils can hardly help feeling that he must be unpractical. They remember the lecture room too well.

It all comes to the same. I have had ideas. Perhaps they are very wonderful ideas. But they will never be worth anything until they have ceased to be my ideas and have become yours. You must take them into your own hands, work them out by your own confidence, not in me, but in them. Perhaps they are unpractical ideas. Then, obviously, it is high time you took someone else with ideas that can be made use of. Here then is my whole point. If the Society does not understand all these ideas, it wants a new leader whom it does understand. If, however, it does realize it all, then it will make them far more effective to itself and others when the purely personal factor is out of the way.

I assume that the Society does accept its ideas. It may still argue it wants my organizing power, it wants my guidance in their fulfilment. I contend it wants nothing of the sort. It has wanted them. It wants now to rush them through. All I can do, I can do much better as a private person. If I am a man of ideas, then I can be chief of intelligence. If I can organize then I can be chief of staff.

Let it be granted that there are things on which my own insight and foresight are still very necessary. Let us say the Baslow policy (S.C.M.)—quite, to my mind, one of the biggest things within our reach. Is it not one of our first principles that the superior is

not the clever man, but the man who uses cleverness? Is there any
reason to believe that the superior you appoint will not know how
to use the powers the Society contains? Is it not the whole essence
of a Society that it should say boldly—'Oh yes, we have big men,
but we use them, not they us'?

I now come to the question of what the Society should or can
do. I want to keep these two questions, 'What is the right thing
for the Society?' and 'How it should be carried out?' clear and
distinct. If you are convinced that it is best for me to be Director,
I shall not persuade you to look further. If you at all share my
convictions, I have already suggested to your chairman five ways
out of the difficulty. I have kept back a sixth way. I want you to
remember and recognize that my whole contention has been that
the Chapter must not merely decide right, but it must so decide
as to carry the whole mind of the Society with it.

It is obvious that a decision might be reached if some representatives, whether of the home or foreign provinces, would act
upon the authority given them and change their votes; but this
fails to meet the situation. It is a doubtful hesitating decision. The
Society must prepare itself for battle, and for that an uncertain
sound is the very last means.

The real difficulty springs from the fact that I have—at least
in the eyes of the Church—allowed my own personality to over-
shadow the real power of the Society. If the Society had been
unanimous in her desire for a new Director, that would have
proved that she was free from that error. But her opinion is not
unanimous. If I persuade some delegates here to change their votes,
the Society will have reached a decision which will be loyally
accepted, but that is not sufficient. If we refer the question back
to the provinces, and I persuade them, that too is not sufficient.
It is another Kelly theory. What good is it if you choose a new
captain, as long as I remain sitting in an easy chair on the quarter-
deck? If I take to the boats, it suggests panic. But I ask your leave
to jump overboard. You can only say 'You can if you like.' You
can fish me out and put me to bed, but the ship is yours now.

I have now for many months past been studying this question
in all its bearings, and so far as I can see there is but one door
left. It is still open to me to demand from the Vicar-General my

release from the Society. If the Society bids me to be Director, no man may fling out of the Society as an alternative to obedience. Nevertheless there the door is. Only I can open it. I may not open it by disobedience, but the Constitution provides that I may open it by permission. If the Vicar-General with your consent—and I refer it to you *ad determinandum*—will grant that release 'with assent,' I intend to apply immediately for admission as a novice as soon as he permits in the usual way.[4]

I meant that proposal in all seriousness. I have gone over it again and again in my own mind. I admit it can look a bit theatrical (is bizarre the right word?), but I thought then—and go on thinking—that the Society missed one of the best opportunities it ever had when it turned the offer down emphatically. I should dearly like to have it made a rule that every superior should begin life again after so much power. However my proposal settled the election question.[5]

Fr. Kelly again refers in the beginning of Chapter IX to the inherent difficulty involved in the position of a Founder, especially after fresh circumstances require a change of command. In retrospect it is difficult to believe that this would have been in any considerable way eased if the Founder's seniority in the Society had been reduced by making his profession date officially from 1912 or thereabouts. Not long after 1919, when Fr. Kelly returned from Japan, the main direction of the Society's policy fell into the hands of those who would still have been his juniors, among the many professed soon after the end of the First World War, some of them men of maturity and experience. In any case the Father Founder would have been the one among the elder brethren whose counsel would have carried most weight, and who was most likely to be hurt, for very natural human reasons, when changes were made of which he disapproved. But even if we think that his proposal to become a junior was based on a misconception of the real nature of the difficulty, it does at least witness to his perception of its importance.

---

[4] *Statement, May 31st, 1910.*
[5] *Autobiography.*

VIII

Information about the beginnings of the 'ecumenical movement' can be found in The Story of the Student Christian Movement *by Tissington Tatlow (1933),* The World's Student Christian Federation, *by Ruth Rouse (1948), and* A History of the Ecumenical Movement, 1517–1948, *edited by Ruth Rouse and S. C. Neill (1954). I myself have said something of Fr. Kelly's part in an article in* The Ecumenical Review *for July 1951. It is important to notice that the first summer conferences of what became the S.C.M. were held at Keswick in 1893–5, in the place of the Keswick Convention, and therefore in an atmosphere strongly impregnated by conservative Evangelicalism. Canon Tatlow's chapter on 'the approach to the Church of England,' shows how difficult it was at first to make contact with High Churchmen. On the other hand it was clearly important that as the movement came to admit questions connected with modern thought and higher criticism, which the conservative Evangelicals were reluctant to face, it should not become wholly identified with Liberal Evangelicalism or Modernism. The Liberal Catholics of the Lux Mundi school, who were striving to build some kind of a bridge between traditional theology and modern philosophy, were also in a certain sense in a middle position between liberal and conservative Evangelicals. The Anglicans in the movement were anxious to heal the breaches between the two ends of the Church of England, and perhaps more especially the Irish among them were concerned with the deeper rift between Protestant and Roman Catholic in their own land. In their desire to be inclusive they were reinforced by the sympathy of John R. Mott of the American Y.M.C.A., who had made friends among the Russian Orthodox in the time of the Russo-Japanese war, and was exceedingly anxious to help young Christians, not only in Orthodox but in Roman Catholic countries, without necessarily alienating them from the traditional and historic churches. Fr. Kelly's role in the movement, to which Canon Tatlow pays notable tribute in several places in his book, was due above all to his theological outlook, which was less liberal than that of the Liberal Catholics, more fundamentally based on a theological understanding of the modern world, rather than on any uneasy synthesis between modern theology and philosophy. At the same time he was willing to learn, and much of his interest in modern philosophy, as well as in the history and theology of the continental Reformation, sprang from friendships made at Baslow and Swanwick. When he went to Edinburgh for the World*

Missionary Conference in 1910, he was more daring than most High Churchmen. The Church Times *was severely critical of Anglican participation, and the S.P.G. representatives, although numerous, had no official status.*

Something should be said of one with whom Fr. Kelly was closely associated in these beginnings. Neville Talbot was the son of E. S. Talbot, Bishop successively of Rochester, Southwark, and Winchester, a friend of Scott Holland and through him of Fr. Kelly from his early days. In 1907 he was a young ordinand at Christ Church, Oxford, just about to begin his theological training at Cuddesdon. From 1909 he was chaplain of Balliol College, and closely associated with the group who in 1912 produced Foundations. *Others in this group who knew Fr. Kelly well were A. E. J. Rawlinson, afterwards Bishop of Derby, and William Temple, whose theological evolution in a more orthodox direction owed much to his influence. Neville Talbot was afterwards Bishop of Pretoria, and at the end of his life vicar of S. Mary's, Nottingham, where his association with S.S.M. was renewed. His close connections with Kelham and Mirfield, where his brother was Superior for many years, and through his father with such men as Bishop Gore and Dean Armitage Robinson, were probably an important factor in loosening the reluctance of Anglo-Catholics to engage in ecumenical ventures in the years immediately before the First World War.*

I think it was in 1907 that Neville Talbot appealed to us and other Anglican colleges to enter the Student Christian Movement. I remember that I answered that I was tremendously interested in Church unity. When we had found something of it, it would be time enough to begin our inter-denominational unity. It was a very stupid answer, which has often been made an excuse for not going on foreign missions. Neville answered that 'it was all very well, but you've got to come just the same.' So we went. I went personally, and some students went, each year from 1908.

It was the first camp held at Baslow. To me, and to us, it was very strange. It was the first time I had ever really come across 'British religion' in its whole representation. And it is a whole, of which the Anglicanisms I knew were only a part. No doubt it was a very chaotic whole; then it must be faced as such. Why is it a chaos?

Faith, belief in God, what can that mean in practice except beliefs, which we might as well call opinions? Love of God—what can that mean in practical life, except a response which we do call religion? We were a chaos, because our opinions did not agree, and our religions were so different, so we ran both around and asked why. I had opinions too. On one occasion I explained them to Mr. Tatlow, by permission, in an empty bell-tent, while the rain threshed in the roof. With his experience of the real issues I expect he was only bored. I do not remember what I said, and I do not think he said anything, which was much the wisest thing he could say.

However the camp wanted an answer, and decided that our religions were all a matter of 'temperament.' I thought that heathen, but I did not say so, which showed I was learning some wisdom. Next year, we had forgotten our temperaments, but most years before the war we had a new word. Occasionally we talked of mysticism. I remember one year when everything was Feeling, and another when it was Experience; another (1912) it was Personality, especially the personality of Jesus, with a wonder whether He was conscious of being God. A chaos is a desperate thing to live in, and we were desperately in earnest to find a way out somewhere.

I make my attempt to describe the psychology, the true 'movement' of the camp, because it is a picture of what is going on all over the world. We had lived our own lives, and tried to understand them. We had made a theory, a mind-view, about life. We knew there were other people who had quite different theories. We made our theories, our views, of what their theories were as counter to our own. When we came to camp, we discovered that other people were not theories, but real living folk, and that their theories were not counters, but had something in them of a real positive life. In a puzzled way we tried to find out what their theories meant to them—not how they argued about them, for we had sense enough not to argue—but how they lived them. There were in the camp two things. There was all this mass of theories, outlooks, ways of taking things. But the camp was in fact a meeting place of what a scientist would call 'forces' which we only dimly apprehended as such. Our theories were attempts to explain whence they came and whither they were going, which it is not easy to do with the Holy Spirit. And we were chaotic; we never did succeed in finding a sure way out because we were trying to find it by manipulating our theories.

But there was one factor about the camp curiously significant. The members were mostly students and changed completely every two or three years. There was a certain proportion of us elders, as guides of youth. We were serious and solemn people, formed in mind, deeply committed, aware of our responsibilities. We could not change our theories. The students had no responsibilities, and did not mind giving things away, or looking at what was new. I do not mean that the young are less cock-sure, less conceited and assertive, than the old. As life gets on, the sense of its vastness and complexity grows on one, just as the power to deal with them grows less. Time is running short, and when one has learnt to see, it is time to go home.[1]

Monday [2] was Missions and Governments. I thought that looked a very stupid subject, so kept out of it. I discovered a nice smoke room on the top floor, where I could go on writing my article, descending at intervals, e.g. lunch time, etc., when I thought there was the best chance of catching interesting people. I didn't make many important new acquaintances, though some, but I renewed many others.

Tuesday was the most exciting day, Co-operation and Unity. There were all sorts of schemes about universal federation, limitation of spheres, exchange of converts, and the like, possible or impossible. Anglicans in a great state of excitement, sure that the last day had come. Excitement all the more because there was talk of a Continuation Committee, which was to operate some sort of something. This time I went and stopped about an hour. There was some wild talk, much more aimlessness, which might of course mean anything. There was, I believe, much better speaking in the afternoon. All the necessary things were said, and I believe the true state of affairs is something like this. The flapdoodle vein is pretty well worked out. Certainly the younger generation are getting rather tired of it. They have heard so often that we are all going the same way that it has ceased to influence them. There is

[1] *Personal Thoughts Concerning Unity.*
[2] Letter to his mother from the World Conference at Edinburgh (June 29th, 1910).

a bit of feeling that since it hasn't come off, there must be something at the back not quite covered. Hence the extraordinary willingness to listen to quite advanced talk and to give it all consideration.

Now comes Wednesday. This was our day, Commission V,
Preparation of Missionaries. I went to breakfast with Principal
Whyte, an exceedingly sweet old don of the Presbyterian school
that was due up about last century but two. Tatlow was there, and
some others. Thence we adjourned to the meeting. Mott was in
the chair. He was very American. I rather wanted to get my oar
in, but didn't know how. However Tatlow told Mott he wanted
me to speak, although it was against the rules, to which Mott
said, 'Wall, I guess we'll get him in.' T.T. (Tatlow) told me afterwards he thought Mott wanted to, so about twelve o'clock I was
called on. I had seven minutes, and used it as well as I could. First
I pitched into theology as she is taught. Christianity was the power
of common life, and it was handled as the mere science of a
religious sphere. Then I got on to the subject of intellectual freedom, which closed the time. My little squirt was fairly well
received. It gave me a sense of reality in the eyes of other people.
I don't know whether this is the object of the Conference, but I
don't see why it shouldn't be. It's the same thing as getting to
know one another.

One word in the Report [3] on which I want to fix your minds is
the word 'knowledge' of Christianity. Christianity is the simplest
thing in the world, and therefore the knowledge of it and its
application in a complex world is bound to be a most complex and
most difficult problem. We assume that we all know Christianity.
Is the thing that we are teaching in our universities, the thing on
which we are examining boys, the things on which we are lectur-
ing—are they the knowledge of Christianity? By the knowledge
of Christianity we mean one thing, and one thing only. I take it
that it is the really clear sight of the revelation of Christ, in the
real actual world in which men live and the life they live in it.
I want to put that in the simplest and most practical kind of way.

[3] World Missionary Conference, 1910, supplement to the Report of Commission V, p. 312 (Fr. Kelly's speech).

Supposing a bank manager asks us who are teachers of theology, what has Christian doctrine ever done for or what has it got to do with my bank? Will anything in your teaching help me to understand my work better or do it with more energy or more purpose? If not, the theology we are teaching in our universities and colleges is not the theology that missionaries want, not the theology that the missionary life requires, and it is not the theology that either you or I want in England. What has all your teaching to do with the life men lead? Is it bringing home those facts, the virgin birth, the resurrection, the cross, throwing light upon the actual life, not that we parsons and ministers are leading, but that the layman is leading with his lay interests and in his work to-day? That is the view of Christianity that we want for the mission field, that the missionaries ask from us, and I cannot help feeling that they hardly seem to imagine how entirely new a thing they are asking, and how little we ourselves have understood it. If we want to teach this Christianity and this knowledge of it, we want enormously more intellectual freedom in our colleges than we have got—perhaps less criticism—more meaning, more thought, and above all, more independence. A man can only think what he thinks himself. He can only learn what God gives him to see. You can only give boys something you imagine you have seen for yourself. They must make what they can of it with their own hearts and their own thinking.

The Edinburgh Conference is now past.[4] What result it may produce in the mission field we have yet to see. The controversy over the action of certain Church Societies will presently come to an end, but the state of anxiety and uncertainty still remain. The Church has taken a momentous step the consequences of which no one can quite foresee. For my part, I am quite convinced that that step was more and not less momentous than is supposed, and at the same time it was quite inevitable. Cautious people, those especially who have to defend their own actions, try very reasonably to show that they have not committed themselves; but the Conference is only one step, one result, one manifestation of an entirely new situation which we were too little prepared to meet.

Hitherto much the larger number of our missionaries have been

4 S.S.M., Q.P., September, 1910.

sent out without any knowledge of heathen religions. We knew very little of them. Yet they must contain the fullest and deepest expression of the native mental character, of what is best as well as what is worst in it. If we understood them, they might at least intimate to us what would be the teaching which the native mind would most readily appreciate. Further, there can be nothing true in them which is not in Christianity, and which does not need Christianity to draw it out, purify and perfect it, but then the infinite richness of Christianity must contain sides to which our Western minds do inadequate justice, which in truth our converts may understand better than we do. By the necessity of our own limitations, we can only be teachers of Western Christianity, but of Christianity itself we are still learners, and he is a very poor teacher who is not glad to learn from his pupils.

Secondly, in regard to ourselves, comes the question of Unity and Co-operation. The spectacle of three or four denominations contending for the possession of a promising convert, or seeking to increase their numbers by bringing over one another's converts—often with very little examination as to the reputation of the proselyte—is enough to make all but the toughest controversialist hesitate. The open scandal of our disagreements has done, is doing, untold mischief to Christianity. The least we can do is to keep it out of sight as much as we can.

Of course with continued growth and expansion this will not long be possible, even where it is possible now. We must face the question of unity soon; we ought to be considering it now. What is to be the Christianity of China or Korea? Will it be divided like our own into a multitude of sects? We may say 'No' to that with reasonable conviction. If it does not reach a unity of some kind, it is very doubtful if it will bear up against western scepticism and materialism. We have been told by very competent observers that Christianity will not make much further progress unless she finds unity. The Conference was told by a native Chinese minister that our divisions did not correspond to anything the Chinese themselves felt, and that if it were not for the European missionaries they themselves would settle their differences very quickly.

This view of the situation would, I believe, be accepted by the leaders of the Conference as representing their own mind. It is

H

such as might have occurred to any one, and has more or less been felt by all thoughtful people. It was suggested that the questions all had to face should be discussed together, and it should be discussion only. All bodies, all societies, would preserve their own freedom of action. No body should be asked to compromise in any way its own beliefs. To the protestant bodies that presents no difficulty. Whatever may have been the case once, the present tendency is to a mutual recognition of one another's position. Co-operation, even Federation, are within reach. Union is at least a possibility.

When however the Church is asked to join, the proposal wants very serious consideration. The very beginning of a 'mutual recognition' lies in the belief that our differences are due only to differences in character, or, to use the popular word, to differences of 'temperament.' Now while we admit that there must always be a great deal which is temperamental—indeed 'Anglicanism' is essentially temperamental—yet the essence of 'the Church' is that it is an order which goes behind the temperamental.

The sacramental Presence is a divine gift, under appointed conditions, ministered by those holding commission from the Apostles for that purpose. This therefore constitutes the Catholic order, the same for all men. The mere forms of administration, all manner of additional services, all which constitutes Anglicanism, we willingly admit to be of secondary importance.

If we were stronger than we are, it might be possible for us to go our own way, and our refusal to co-operate might be a very serious matter. My own feeling is very strong that we are within measurable distance of a great movement, and, as things are, if we stand aside it will go forward quite effectively without us. Any one who has enjoyed the luxury of sulking knows how pleasant it is to maintain one's own dignity behind a strict reserve, and knows also how annoyingly unconscious other people can be of one's absence.

Let us consider what our old policy has been, and what it has done for us. We held to a God-given unity and order in a Church, One, Catholic, and Apostolic and to a God-given grace of the sacrament in that Church, as matters of positive truth. This claim was opposed to the whole weight of nineteenth century feeling,

its love of pure individualism in which each man is free to make
his own way, associate or dissociate himself with or from any one
he chooses. In such a current it was hardly possible to do more
than take up a protestant attitude, refusing to join in any action
not based on our principle. If we could not stem the current, at
least we kept the principle intact.

This rigid attitude, if it has its advantages, has also its weaknesses. It may be a necessary defensive policy, but it is not an
effective teaching, and if it saves our principles, it will not do much
to save the world.

It is a military principle of great value everywhere, that nothing
destroys the spirit of an army so quickly as taking refuge in a
fortress. That is exactly what we have found. We cannot trust our
own people, not even our own leaders. I do not think any one
can doubt that it is not fear of what others may do, but uncertainty whether our own representatives will stand fast, which is the
root of all our anxiety—a natural and well-grounded anxiety. Let
us, however, take a lesson from Christianity. We have been told
by the heathen abroad, and by many at home who do not like to
be called heathen, that we should settle our own differences, con-
vince our own unbelievers, before we undertook missions. Once
on a time we tried it. The heathen waited while we jangled and
argued endlessly. At last earnest men cried out, 'Christianity is a
Gospel. It wants preaching more than proving.' So we took our
Christianity in our hands, somewhat faded and very tattered, but
it was all we had to give. And behold, when we gave it, it grew
bright and living; it began to prove itself. Most wonderful of all,
it is beginning to grow a new wholeness.

This also was the most wonderful thing at Edinburgh. There
were a number of us who were by no means inclined to give great
value to institutional forms. There were many who were naturally
inclined to minimize differences, to fall back upon the comfortable
'we-are-all-going-the-same-way' style of talking, especially in the
early stages. But as we got to know other people better, as we got
to realize their actual position, just so far we all began to realize
better our own position, and the value of what God had given to
us. In the actual discussion on unity, it was extraordinary, not
merely how little minimizing there was, but how little weight it

carried. Those who spoke most clearly and emphatically were generally recognized as the most genuine exponents of the Church's position. Those who listened might not be ready to accept it themselves, but they did accept it as a statement of the position to be met. I hesitate to say it, and yet the impression left on my mind was that they realized that it was a position which would have to be accepted ultimately as the only final solution.

We do well to believe in the Church, but that is not the same as believing in our notion of it. In regard to the Church as in regard to Christianity if we have a great deal to give we have also a great deal to learn. As one as in the other, it is a very dangerous thing to allow ourselves or others to think or feel that they have to submit to us on the terms we assign.

To get this question on to a true and possible basis, I would ask consideration for two suggestions.

First, are not words like 'surrender' and 'submission' here somewhat misleading? We are not asking any one to 'surrender' anything. We are asking others to realize, to learn something which is necessary to the preservation, permanence, fulfilment, of that which they already hold. In the true sense of the word, no doubt, learning always involves at least submissiveness, as to a truth greater than knowledge. In the common use, however, submission suggests the acceptance of a whole idea upon adequate reason or authority. Learning on the other hand always implies long testing, criticism, a gradual entry into the true sense of what is to be learnt.

What do we ourselves mean by the Church? If we have any vital consciousness of it as a tremendous power that holds us, surely we must recognize that that consciousness can only be reached by others very slowly as each man can see his way, very slowly as it takes hold also of him. If we think of it merely as the theory which we hold, then it may be natural to expect others to be readily convinced that it is a very fine theory. Of course we do not mean to think of the Church only as our theory, but are we sure we are not unconsciously so regarding the matter?

Secondly, wherever there is a quarrel people will ask whether there are not faults on both sides. We have no excuse for quarrelling, but there are differences, and we have every reason to ask whether there are not weaknesses and losses on both sides. Look where we will, on the Continent, in the mission field, at home, is it not the cause of all our weakness that what God meant as complementary, men have treated as antithetical? And the righteousness of God has been fulfilled in judgment. The forms, reft of the spirit, have stiffened into death; the spirit, unstayed by form, continually dissolves into states of our own feeling. But Thou, O Lord, have mercy upon us. Wilt Thou not turn again and quicken us, that Thy people may rejoice in Thee?

England is a small island. We cannot get so far away from one another as on a roomy continent, therefore we quarrel more, but also we are more influenced by one another. The division is less complete, and the phenomena are more complex. Yet in degree the same is true. The Church is less rigid, has more freedom and movement, but is still distressingly wooden, cautious, lacking in enthusiasm and leadership. There is no better test of spiritual vitality than foreign missions, and there our own inferiority shows how much we have to learn.

Our greatest danger at the present time is Inter-Denominational Federation, and these ways of getting rid of practical inconveniences are altogether too easy and too human. Surely our disunion arises because there is something we have failed to learn, and if so, Unity will be found by learning more of the Unity God makes, not by going back to something of man's devising. Either our beliefs mean something to us, or they do not. Once federated, either we break up the unity by asserting them, or we learn to abandon them as of secondary importance. The latter course is almost inevitable, but where is this retrograde movement to stop? Some urge on us that all dogmatic belief is secondary.

At Edinburgh we were all select delegates, very much grown up, with the responsibilities of a representative position. It was no wonder we were cautious; it was very wonderful that we were so daring, with what courage we could look questions in the face. It must be for the coming generation really to deal with them. Young nations abroad, young people at home, are earnestly inquiring what is to come next. Now that God is moving even us, still more them, He cannot mean this futile separation to go on much longer. Can we not look to our children to set their face towards

the new world of peace and worship? Ought we not to go gladly
to meet them, leaving behind our dignities and infallibilities that
they also may lay aside their impatience and self-confidence, for
with God we are all nothing more than children?

> Fear God and give glory to Him
> For the hour of His judgment is come.

In 1912 [5] I wrote a book on Unity. Just as we, Catholics or
Protestants, are confused over a dualism of authority and freedom,
so we are confused by the dualism of acts and feelings. In fact,
both are our own; both, so far, may be self-worship. Yet Evangelicalism is committed utterly to salvation as an act of God, of
Christ. And Evangelicalism will never maintain itself steadily till
its worship also shall turn itself primarily on the sacrament—not
as an act of man, or even of the Church, which it so easily becomes
—but as an act of God, given to man and the Church; till we take
it as a sacrifice, not because it is an act, but because it is surrender.

Early in 1912 I went on a short visit with Neville Talbot to
America, to try and persuade the American Episcopal Colleges to
join in the movement there. Certainly it was by now abundantly
clear that if the Catholic Church had a gift, she must find out
what it was and give it. I doubt if we effected anything, but I, at
least, learnt a great deal. Before the book was out, I was already
wondering whether I had reached the real difficulty. After all, the
camp in general (sc. S.C.M.) was not in the old sense 'Evangelical.'
Students, if anything, were modern. 'God so loved the world,'
but when we thought of the world, we did not think of God;
we thought of our moral duty towards social problems. 1912 was
to be my last camp, and I think it was here I began to throw about
what seemed to me the vital challenge—What does God do? Does
He Himself do anything? Is He more than a name for an ideal,
an excuse for emotions, a sanction for betterments, where our
Idealisms, efforts, activities, subjectivities and experiences are what
really matter?

In many ways [6] the situation is extraordinarily hopeful. The

---

[5] *Personal Thoughts Concerning Unity.*

[6] *The Present Condition of Theological Movement in America,* a paper
presented to J. R. Mott on April 24th, 1912.

whole country is feeling the impulse of a wave of religious seriousness. The universities are feeling it. Of course there are many
dangers implied in that movement, and—as we have only too much
reason to see in Wales—the scale and enthusiasm of any wave
movement makes its dangers all the greater. I lay stress on these
dangers not out of a desire to be critical, but because they need
facing.

We are rather apt to forget that the central question of religion
is concerned with the relation of man to God. Is there such a thing
as God? Is He actually the ruler of the world, or are human ideas,
purposes, efforts, activities the only true factors of life? Christianity is not a new Jesus-worship: it is solely concerned with
the Revelation of God to man, and the reconciliation of man to
God in Christ.

Old-fashioned Protestants had in practice a very vivid perception of this principle. They were full of the conviction of human
worthlessness and sinfulness, yet by their simple minded faith in
God and in what God would do through and in them, they
achieved great victories, moral and other, without ever thinking
of themselves in the matter.

The old faith in God, in the redemption He has worked for man,
and is working, has now almost disappeared. Sir Oliver Lodge
gives the classical expression—'the modern man is not worrying
about his sins. His business is to be up and doing.' Very few
religious people would accept so blunt a statement, but this is
just the danger. We do not care to formulate our meaning, and
in consequence we are drifting into it without knowing.

At one university I find a whole mixed committee (churchmen
and all) full of the sweetest earnestness and prayerfulness, humble
and contrite Christians, visibly resting all that they do on God,
yet when they got talking of their Y.M.C.A. work, you would
not imagine that they had ever heard of a God in heaven or on
earth. They were just full of their own activities: they would set
God's world straight for Him. It would have such an excellent
effect on their own character, and doing it made you feel ever so
nice.

But supposing I grant that these boys were so beautifully good
and Christian, what does their somewhat defective theological

expression matter? To them, as they are just now, nothing at all. But there are two other ways where it matters a great deal.

The boys whom I met were just the picked devotionalists of their university, who had—I do not doubt—pious and loving homes. I believe it to be the great defect of this pietism that it has no idea how entirely it depends on a certain religious emotionalism. What could that touching sweetness mean to the ordinary student, who is thinking how to push his way unfriended in a very hard and practical world?

As a mere visitor to this country, one is confronted even more than in England with the question—what has the Crucifixion to say to all this roaring energy of civilization and to those caught up in it. And it is a strange thing that with all our 'Social-problems-Christianity' which is talked on all sides, and head-lined in every paper, the very idea that God and His Christ is concerned in man's daily work, in its efficiency, in its conduct, in one's relation with those around, the elevator man, the shoe-shine boy, in the relations between the manufacturer and his employees, hardly seems to enter our heads.

The time is not far off when the psychologists will show that this God who is known only to a religious experience is merely a name for certain mental states. (James shrank back from this conclusion somewhat inconsistently.) Surely if God can do nothing in His own universe, if He has left it to purely human activity to make the best of it, who is He even to be judge at last? ('God has never yet had a fair chance with the world.' The Swanwick speaker went on to explain—apparently—that we were to get it straight for Him. 'God must be almost broken-hearted at the way things are going'—so an Anglican divine.) It was somewhat ominous that this Y.M.C.A. group worked in perfect harmony on all practical questions with an 'Ethical section' formed on a non-religious basis.

How has this change been brought about, and how is it possible that people should be so unconscious of it? These are two questions, but intimately connected with each other. The change has come about, or is coming about, mainly because people are unconscious of it. The real beginning of the move was excellently expressed by a *very* senior secretary to whom I had been pointing out the drift from 'faith to works,' i.e. from God to self. He admitted it, but explained it as 'the swing of the pendulum,' 'Formerly men did talk a great deal of faith, but they have learnt to see that we cannot go so exclusively upon our feelings. Things have swung over—perhaps too far—to what we have to do.'

I would take this as a text. The old Protestantism began with faith in God. There were works to be done, but what they did was so dominated by this trust in God that they hardly thought of it as their own. God worked in them and through them, and they left the result to God in peace and confidence.

The theological and quasi-credal basis of this faith has dropped out (I should say because of the absence of any effective and permanent presentation of it in religious worship, i.e. sacraments). Whatever the reason may be, it has dropped or is dropping out. The faith still maintained itself, but it began to be recognized as a feeling—a 'feeling of assurance.' Now faith is an attitude of looking for something other than ourselves. It may manifest itself in feelings of assurance, as also in doing things, or in not doing them, but it is not in itself either a feeling or an activity. This confusion has in fact led men to substitute faith-in-feelings-about-God for faith in God Himself. Then the door is opened to faith in activities, and God drops out much more obviously.

When one gets into the thinking student world (seminaries and large universities), or into the practical world of business in the large cities, or into the religious world of the smaller towns where people are not weighted with official responsibilities, then you get their true mind. All denominational differences are admitted to be meaningless, and all positive faith goes under various opprobrious epithets as 'theological' or 'dogmatic.' One section of this movement is *aggressively* modernist, self-satisfied. I cannot call it other than definitely anti-Christian in any sense in which the word Christian has yet been held. It holds an active propaganda of a new Gospel, which it still calls Christian.

The main body is not, however, anti-Christian in any formal sense. It is only utterly ignorant of what is at stake or how to find any solid ground. Just because of its ignorance it is easily satisfied with any kind of religiousness, and with anything that calls itself Christian. As usual, those who do not know what they want fall easy victims to those who do. Men are carried by the momentum of the crowd, and never dream of asking critically whether it knows where it is going.

In speaking of this as the actual aspect of 'the movement,' do I mean that this is the result of the Y.M.C.A. movement? This is an exceedingly difficult question to answer. I might evade it by saying that my actual business here is to explain how Y.M.C.A. strikes churchmen. To them, at least to the clergy with their credal and other forms, the drift is plain enough. They see it going on in young America, and this young America of the non-Episcopalian bodies clusters round the Y.M.C.A. The churchman therefore regards what I have called 'the movement' as a Y.M.C.A. movement, though of course he will recognize that there are more conservative elements. A young Episcopalian seminarist asked us straight out, 'Is the Y.M.C.A. Christian?' And it is this feeling that holds them back from co-operation.

I do not think it was possible to say simply 'yes.' We could say that the Y.M.C.A. meant to be Christian, and that its leaders were most anxious that it should be. But its wide circle represents 'American religion as she is held.' Within that circle there are immensely powerful non-Christian forces. I do not think that their power, their subtlety of infiltration, their silent attractiveness, are in general at all adequately realized. In other words, this drift is not the work of the Y.M.C.A. movement, but it is taking place in it. It is the field in which they show themselves, and in which therefore they can be met.

I do not see that the Y.M.C.A. can do much more than it is doing. It is not a Church. It cannot amplify its theology, or undertake prosecutions for heresy. These 'un-Christian' movements are inconsistent with the Y.M.C.A. basis, but the Y.M.C.A. cannot do more to shut them out. It would destroy its own character, and the value of its own work, if it did. The Y.M.C.A. must first realize that a tremendous battle is going on, which will have to be fought out. Just because the Y.M.C.A. is not a Church, just because it has this representative character, just because it cannot take sides, it seems to be one part of God's special calling, that it should be the field where that battle will be most effectively fought out. The battle-ground of unity and the battle-ground of Christianity must of necessity be the same, if the unity is to be Christian.

Y.M.C.A.

There are a multitude of voices assuring it that there is no battle at all, and that apart from a few insignificant Episcopalians, impossible R.C.s, fossil theologians and the like, we are all agreed. In crowds of local centres this easy-going notion prevails. In the conferences generally there is (so we are given to understand) a certain feeling of resentment that any one ringing a theological firebell is disturbing the peace.

I only want to point out how important it is that the Y.M.C.A. should stick very definitely to the genuineness of its interdenominationalism. The general Y.M.C.A. position and traditions are so near undenominationalism, and the undenominational tradition of 'Oh, let's stick to what we are agreed about' is so attractive, that there is real need that the centre should use its influence, so far as it can go, with the authorities that that is not the true Y.M.C.A. principle. Every one who is conscious of having a doctrine ought to be able to feel that so long as he acts reasonably, he has the higher authority of the Movement behind him. If the Y.M.C.A. should at this crisis try to suppress, or should the advocates of peace succeed in repressing, the expression of differences, the result can lead to nothing but the minimizing of all beliefs whatever.

To my first paper on the state of religion in America Mott entirely assented. It was a remarkable thing that he should have so entirely seen exactly what things meant.

The 'comment on the invitation to ourselves to undertake the tour' [7] by Neville Talbot Mott entirely endorsed, and has given

---

[7] 'We have had to account for something of a modern miracle, viz. the touring of the U.S.A. by Father Kelly (not without his red girdle) as a delegate of the Student Y.M.C.A. . . .

'We have had to give our surmises:

'(1) That Mr. Mott has been impressed by the effect of Anglican contributions to the British Student Movement.

'(2) We have found that there are a number of Episcopalians in general universities who do co-operate with Y.M.C.A. and who do go to Conferences, but who do so in such a way as to be practically swallowed up and to have their distinctive colour washed out of them by the general tide of Y.M.C.A. religion. This has therefore strengthened our belief that what Mr. Mott is after is that the difficult task (difficult all round in U.S.A.) of Episcopalianism making itself felt as such should be attempted.

'(3) We have looked for a further explanation in the direction of the Federation. We have pictured Mr. Mott as in touch with the problem of students in Roman and Greek (not to say Coptic) Catholicism. We have said that we believed that in dealing, say, with Russian students, his hope is not to me authority to show it round as a statement of his view.[8]

separate them from their national Church, not to make Protestants of them, but to bring them through the W.S.C.F. the stimulus which it has to give them, in order that that stimulus may work with renovating and purifying influence on the old and immobile body of Russian Catholicism.

'We have also said that we believed that Mr. Mott sees what we believe we see to some extent, viz. that two main elements of Christianity lie at present apart (call them Catholicism and Evangelicalism or Protestantism): that apart and in divorce both elements are the prey of the defects inherent in their qualities and excellencies . . .: that the two sides must come together for either's sake if Christianity is to deal with its world task.

'Hence we believed sprang Mr Mott's interest in the contribution of Anglicanism to the Student Movement, it being some sort of meeting place between the two extremes, in that, in a confused way, it holds together both Catholicism and Protestantism in one body.'

[8] *American diary.*

124

IX

The excuse for my offer in 1910 was to get over a technical difficulty. I very much wanted to do it for my own soul's sake, but
the main reason was to make an act of faith in the Society, and
perhaps to show what a man's attitude should be towards status
and authority. There is a plain gospel teaching about being 'first,'
and among crowds of exceedingly sincere Christian people, I hardly
know any one who does not feel hurt, bitterly hurt, at being 'deposed'—which I should have expected would be a joyous bit of
fun. I wanted to show it.

I had another practical reason. For twenty years I had held a
unique position, to which no one could succeed. Now the Society
was to have a head of its own choosing. Cowley, with obvious
common sense, shipped Father Benson off to Boston, but there
was nowhere my uselessness could go. Stopping in the House,
would it be possible for me to say anything, to give advice, to use
what ability I might have—without making people jealous and
resentful of 'interference'?

I believed I had enough reputation to get a job somewhere for
a time. I went to America in 1912. I tried India. Then suddenly
an offer came from Japan. It has always been a satisfaction to me
that I never held an appointment that any one else would touch;
consequently, I never blocked the way of a better man. This was
the first and only time of my life I was actually asked to do something. There was a new theological college just starting. Bishop
Cecil engineered the invitation; the other bishops were afraid of
me. They took an early opportunity of being very rude. Probably I
ought to have bitten them, but did not. That, however, went for
nothing.

Too, the whole situation was novel to a degree. After that first
silliness no one said, 'Who the dickens are you?' and no one was
jealous of me. The Japanese Christian world was a very small
affair with nobody of more than third-rate status, although amongst
ourselves there were grades. I think our people were all fourth-
rate, less highly (or less pretentiously) educated than the U.S.A.
men. A man who really had ideas was a wonder, even if he was

only a second-rater. When he laughed profusely at the idea of having a status, of which they thought such a lot, they wondered still more.

The College system was quite impossible, and quite impossible to alter. My beloved Imai, the Principal, offered to put the whole teaching under my direction. I had been there before, and was not taking any. The bishops would never have allowed it. I said if the staff could follow my ideas, they would do it for themselves; they certainly would not at my directions. The staff, in fact, were American trained and had not the least idea of teaching. There was no real discipline, and the students went preaching all Sundays. I told them what I thought of things, and started to teach. The Japanese suffer from an inferiority complex, and are proportionately touchy. I insisted this was their country and their Church; 'I was only a foreigner.' My very helplessness was a help—notably my ignorance of the language. I paraded it laughing. They knew they were not clever, but they resented the missionaries pushing them. So we got on very well. They are supposed to be hard to understand; my impression is that they are hard to understand because they are much simpler than we are.

The position was comprehensible enough. Their character is astonishingly simple; their mental education is Buddhist, which gives them rather a (very un-English) liking for abstract philosophy. Mentally our people fed them with (S.P.G.) High Church orthodoxies and forms which they accepted in a bewildered way, and with (C.M.S.) Evangelical orthodoxies which they also accepted without understanding; for there are very few genuinely 'evangelical' Japanese. The American protestant sects fed them with modernisms, resting on criticism and a distant backwash of Harvard idealism (Hegelian)? They did not in the least know what it meant, but it was the very latest thing; it looked clever (that appeals to people who are not) and superior to the orthodoxy of old-fashioned traditionalism. The split between the educated ('high collar') and simple is very marked. They were hungering for something solid which they could understand. Our own people were anti-modernist, but they knew nothing about it, least of all about Hegel; consequently, they could not answer it.

I had been through all this for myself years ago, and I was in

my element. I laughed at the fine language which attracted them
so much, imitated it, made them see its absurdity, and brought
them back to the plain issues of faith in the reality of God. I threw
my best Maurician Catholicism about in all directions, for I was
asked to Summer Schools, and other functions. Of course, they had
had explanations and arguments in crowds, but real 'meanings' in
my sense of the word (whatever that might be) were quite new to
them. All sorts of people whom I'd never seen took up whatever ideas I had to give, quietly, in their own fashion, as they
could see their way—which was just what I wanted—and no one
said, 'What does Fr. Kelly mean?'

Did they 'agree' with me? It was part of my joy that I never,
but once, heard the word mentioned. A certain Japanese to whom
I had been talking about the Apocalypse said, 'Oh, you are a
paulo-post preterist. I take the *ex post facto* view.' I have got the
terms wrong, though I think I had heard them before. They never
meant much to me, and I never remember them, but the Apocalypse has meant a great deal. This sort of thing was very rare.
As a rule they just wanted to learn as much as they could, which is
exactly what I always wanted to do myself.

One thing I did not quite like. I fought hard against the snare
of personal influence, against 'Kellyism' or the idea that I was
putting up peculiar opinions. But they would have it that way.
The 'chela' stunt (see *Kim*—we call it 'deshi'—disciple) is a recognized national habit. I believe there is a 'Kelly Association' to this
day. I do not think it does them harm in fact.

I played the same game on the American Protestants where I
could, and they also fell to it. They were desperately solemn about
their personality worship, character building, uplift, and so on.
I had always seen (you cannot go on studying reality without seeing) the absurdities of phraseology. I made fun of it, and they
rocked with laughter. It speaks volumes for their genuineness that
no one, to my knowledge, took offence at it. It was in Japan,
I think, that I first really learnt the power of laughing and making
people laugh with you. You must laugh at yourself first, it is a very
good antiseptic for vanity.

Of course I had to keep off the controversial 'strong points' with
their barbed wire. Once I gave four addresses at Karuizawa on the

Trinity, and the reality of God. I had them separated from Evensong. I was told, 'The missionaries (C.M.S.) went out and the hotel people (and Union Chapel) came in.' I made 'a deep impression' (the newspapers said so). Two U.S.A. missionaries left their sects and joined the Church. Of course they said nothing to me about it. It was just how I like to have it. Anyhow, like it or not, it is the way things happen to me.

As is also usual with me, I got on least well with our own people. The S.P.G. and C.M.S. were carrying on an age-long quarrel. The summer is trying to English folk, and every year they used to get up a solemn protest about something. The S.P.G. were annoyed at me because I would not join in. What was the possible use? The C.M.S. were also not quite pleased: it was not playing the game because I would not be quarrelled with. There is a lot of self-importance about that passion for differing, but I had games of my own to play, and it was part of my game not to admit a schism between us. Of course I never dare poke fun at either of these parties.

There was never anything like this in my life. For once I really could think I had been effective but if any one asks me what I think I effected and whether it really came to anything. of course I cannot tell. It seemed to, and that tickled my vanity egregiously. It is no wonder that I long to go back, even though I am quite conscious that I ate as much jam as was good for my foolish soul—and a bit more. I suspect also I was in Japan as long as was good for them. I am a memory. If I had stopped longer I might probably have become a bore.[1]

The vital point is that the Japanese people suffer from an inferiority complex.[2] They are very ambitious, full of pluck, but at the same time conscious that their abilities are not equal to their desires. They have the self-consciousness of the artistic temperament. This makes them very annoying to the English temperament. I never could see why. I think it fatuous gritting at people as God made them. I was supposed to have an unusual knowledge of

[1] *Autobiography.*
[2] A letter of February 5th, 1934, to the Reverend L. Rose, now Dean of the General Theological Seminary, New York, but then at work in Japan.

Japanese character. I knew nothing at all except as above, and I prefaced everything with the remark: 'I am only a foreigner.' I said it to myself until I meant it; for it is perfectly plain it is their country; only what they do matters. We have a lot to teach them but they will learn it only in their own way.

One consequence you always have to remember; no Japanese will ever admit that he doesn't understand; you have to watch and go on till he does. But another consequence is important—to my mind they are extraordinarily simple; if they like you, and when they do understand, they take it as you give them. They do not, like us folk, go wondering whether they will or won't.

The Japanese mind has three strata. The bottom foundation is the feudal, *samurai* (knightly) loyalty, which is their ideal. It is military, and like all military minds essentially practical, i.e. simple. Beyond those ideals all their fundamental thought is Buddhist, i.e. idealistic. It is an important fact that the best Buddhist 'ordinands' are sent to Kyoto to study Hegelian idealism (I found two of them at Oxford). They are not really idealist or philosophical though they think they are and are very interested. The morality is Chinese Confucianism, platitudinous, with a strong family feeling.

On the top of that they have taken with enthusiasm to western ideas. About everything they must be up-to-date, although they very partially understand it. The result is extremely muddling. Theologically they are modernists, rather wild on higher criticism, although really they have no grasp at all of that attention to minute facts on which it is based; they only like talking about and assuming the results. They have an absurd craze for the American character building, cult of personality, etc., although their feudal instinct is, of course, all against it. In the result, their education is an appalling sham. The medical schools are very good; engineering fairly; military work very scientific; these are the things in which reality cannot be shirked. Their literature, etc., is all talk.

When I went out they said to me, as they have said to you, 'You are to be professor for apologetic theology.' I wrote to my own bishop: 'They can just call it what they please. I am going to try to get these boys to know what a Christian faith means. I have not the remotest intention of defending the faith. My faith

I

has got to defend me. I want to be quite sure what it is, what it can do for me. Of course, I must know all the difficulties in the way, and all the heresies. But they are not somebody else's difficulties and objections, they are mine, yours, the boys'; the difficulties and unbeliefs, etc., in me, in everybody, which the Gospel has come to meet.'

What precisely was the attraction of Fr. Kelly for the Japanese mind? In the memoir attached to the new edition of The Gospel of God *(S.C.M., 1959, p. 28), I quoted from his American diary (1912): 'When I get into these blanked pulpits . . . I can no more keep off rhetorical fireworks than I can keep off rocks when I see 'em. And for all solid purposes they are about equally useful. Every one is filled with admiration as they watch you wriggling out of impossible positions. . . . The wild cheers are given solely for what they take to be your cleverness. What you mean goes for nothing.' Those who have read books on Zen Buddhism will know that the sight of a sage 'wriggling out of impossible positions' is familiar and congenial to the Japanese. Fr. Kelly's message had a profound positive content, in contrast to that of the Zen teachers, whose methods are intended to produce a conviction of total ignorance. ' "Everything ends in mystery, and I call it Buddha," said a monk to a friend of mine,' Fr. Kelly wrote to the Revd. L. Rose (February 14th, 1934). But the element in Fr. Kelly's method of presentation that appeared to English and American audiences as paradoxical, destructive, and at the same time too absurd to be quite serious, commanded attention in Japan. Whether the Japanese altogether understood him, or he them, is another question. On this there might well be more than one opinion.*

EPILEGOMENA

EDITORIAL EPILOGUE

Fr. Kelly 'came back to something very different' in 1919. How different, he did not attempt to explain. Perhaps he never could. At fifty-nine he had already been for some years 'the old man,' and he grew really old very soon. His deafness increased as he explained in Chapter II: 'Till about 1920 I had not much difficulty in private conversation. I was only lost in company.' After this conversation became increasingly difficult. He continued to lecture and to invite questions, crossing the room to answer them. He was always glad when someone came to see him in his room to ask a further question, or to put a difficulty. But his own means of communication, when he had anything important or difficult to say to a superior or to a fellow-tutor, was a long screed generally written on paper manufactured for the purpose of wrapping margarine, and rescued as so much else that might otherwise be wasted was sedulously saved, for instance small pieces of soap, that were refashioned into substantial cakes, other people's safety razor blades, endlessly resharpened, and the backs of old envelopes. What was contained in the screeds frequently tried the patience of those who had much other business, while Fr. Kelly always had plenty of time for his side of the correspondence; but it was always stimulating, and often contained a pithy phrase that went to the heart of the matter in hand, even if he did not always see the other side.

To the end of his life he continued to read and to make notes on old and new books. His lectures showed that in an important sense he was remarkably alive to new ideas, and prepared to abandon old ones. His views on periods of church history, especially the Reformation and the Methodist movement, changed a great deal after 1920. He was also interested in new developments in physical science, in Einstein, and in the more popular books addressed to the general public by Jeans and Eddington. But in another sense he did not change, and many changes round him he never saw in focus. His struggle with Idealism, in the philosophic

131

and in the popular sense, continued long after Oxford Hegelianism had ceased to be an important influence. I do not think that he ever took much notice of Bertrand Russell or G. E. Moore, or of later developments in the analysis of language. He left such things to his brother, Fr. Alfred, whose interest was acute but less sympathetic than his own might have been if he had entered into the full significance of the new Realism. Idealism in the wider sense he knew to be declining. He was not surprised; he had expected this, but he could be shocked at the irreverence of some of the brethren towards the idea of inevitable progress. To doubt the benefit of industrial change, or the goodness of science, was in his eyes a kind of blasphemy against the purpose of God.

This, I believe, coloured his estimate of the reaction against liberalism in philosophy and life which gathered force in the nineteen-twenties. He himself had contributed to it, but he did not like it. He had always stood a little apart from the main stream of the Anglo-Catholic movement through his debt to Kingsley and Maurice. His differences with the Anglo-Catholic party were accentuated by his interest in the ecumenical movement before 1914, and intensified by developments that followed the First World War. Chaplains to the forces had then discovered how deep was the gulf between the Church of England and the whole nation, not only the labouring classes, and how little 'C. of E.' might mean to the man who wore the label because he was not a Roman Catholic, a Free Churchman, or a self-conscious agnostic. Many of the most zealous of the younger clergy, and some of their elders, like Bishop Gore, wished to divide the nation into loyal churchmen and the unevangelized without the fold, or (in Evangelical circles) into converted Christians and unbelievers. The sharp distinction between converted and unconverted, which in Fr. Kelly's youth had been the mark of Evangelical pietism, seemed to him to be pervading the whole field of English organized religion. He wrote in a lecture on Methodism: 'The common Anglo-American idea of religion is to this day fundamentally that of Wesley. We have the same sharp division between the religious and the irreligious. Conversion is the step in which people pass from the one to the other. There is a "method" (observance) which is to maintain the life, as Wesley thought, or which *constitutes* the life, as many of

SECULARITY OR PIETISM?

Wesley's followers supposed that to mean. The method employed differs widely with different schools, but the general principle is the same. Even those who believe themselves to be following Ultramontane pietism borrow only what can be fitted into this framework.' In another place he wrote: 'Wesley came back to Oxford. By some unfortunate blunder the name over his door was J. H. Newman.' [1]

Fr. Kelly still asserted that most people believed 'odd times.' He would have sympathized with T. S. Eliot when he wrote at a rather later date: 'A society has not ceased to be Christian until it has become positively something else. It is my contention that we have to-day a culture which is mainly negative, but which, so far as it is positive, is still Christian. . . . I believe that the choice before us is between the formation of a new Christian culture, and the acceptance of a pagan one. Both involve radical changes; but I believe that the majority of us, if we could be faced immediately with all the changes which will only be accomplished in several generations, would prefer Christianity.' [2]

If this was true in 1939 it was true in 1919, but the issue was then even more confused than it later became by the wide spread of a kind of diffused Christianity which Fr. Kelly himself had denounced, and was still denouncing, as practically pagan. He knew that this had no staying power and that in such places as the Student Christian Movement the battle against a merely liberal Protestantism, although it still continued, was in effect won. He was more apprehensive that the alternative might be pietism among the orthodox, and mere secularity in the world without. Therefore, perhaps, he was inclined to underestimate the theological element in the Anglo-Catholic movement. He hardly perceived the presence of a new theological debate between a deeper and better informed Thomism and the revived theology of the Reformation. He was aware of Barth, and of resemblance and difference between his theology and his own. But he never systematically studied him as he did Luther, and, to a lesser extent, Calvin.[3]

[1] *The Gospel of God* (1959), p. 135; cf. *supra*, p. 93.
[2] *The Idea of a Christian Society*, 1939, p. 13.
[3] In a letter of February 14th, 1934: 'If you want a name, I am called a Barthian. N.B. I never read Barth—I am an F.D. Maurician. I have been preaching that for forty years or more, long before Barth.'

Through Fr. Gabriel Hebert he knew more of developments in Lutheran, and especially Swedish theology, and something of the liturgical movement in the Roman Catholic Church. But I do not think that he ever realized that the new theological movement for which he had hoped and prayed at the time of *Ad Fratres* (1906; cf. pp. 91–5) had actually made some considerable progress, on the continent and in the English Church. Others recognized his influence. When Dr. Visser t'Hooft said of him, that he 'comes perhaps nearer to combining in his life and teaching all that is best of Catholicism and Protestantism than any other Christian alive,' I believe that he was thinking of the influence, not only of Fr. Kelly, but of Kelham and of the S.S.M., on those who were learning at one and the same time from Brunner and Barth, Aulen and Brilioth, and other Protestant theologians, and from Roman Catholic theologians and liturgists, without becoming Barthians or Thomists. When in *Anglo-Catholicism and Orthodoxy* (1933), he appreciated the Anglo-Catholic contribution to the ecumenical movement as serving to promote future contacts, not only with Eastern Orthodoxy, but with Rome, he was thinking of, among others, Fr. Tribe, whose work for the Christian Social Council was well known to him, and Fr. Hebert, who was then completing his translations of Swedish theology, and turning in the new direction that in 1936 produced *Liturgy and Society*.

I would suggest that Fr. Kelly's contribution to the theological movement of this time is most clearly seen, by a curious paradox, in a book where his name is mentioned only once (but in an important place [4]), Dr. John Baillie's *The Idea of Revelation in Recent Thought* (1956). Much of this book is concerned with permutations, variations, and attempted qualifications in the idea of revelation through events, through God's mighty acts, not through propositions or even inspired thoughts. As William Temple put the point: 'The typical locus of revelation is not the mind of the seer but the historical event.' [5] His debt to Fr. Kelly in this matter is emphasized by Professor Dorothy Emmet in her chapter on Temple's philosophy in F. A. Iremonger's biography of the Archbishop.[6] But on the point at issue Fr. Kelly himself denied,

[4] p. 33.
[5] In *Nature, Man, and God*, 1934, p. 318.
[6] *William Temple*, Oxford, 1948, p. 332.

not his influence, but his originality. He gave the credit to 'the
greater portion of Christian history,' and held that 'the tendency
to look on the sacred books as strings of authoritative statements
only came in with the growth of legalistic interests in the Western
Church.' [7] Professor Emmet notes that Fr. Victor White, O.P.,
made a similar criticism of Temple's interpretation of the teaching
of S. Thomas Aquinas in his address to the Aquinas Society in
1943.[8] The professional theologians have been inclined to confine
revelation through events to the acts recorded in the inspired
Scriptures. Probably the most original and distinctive element in
Fr. Kelly's thinking lay in his insistence that what God is doing
could and should be seen in the whole course of history. He saw
the judgments of God on the whole history of the Church from the
thirteenth century onwards in the break-up of the unity of Christen-
dom at the Reformation. God has shut us up into schism, that in
His own time He may have mercy upon us all.

On this matter some of his aphorisms might be acceptable to
Roman Catholic thinkers. 'S.Thomas left the door ajar, Duns Scotus
pushed it open, and Ockham walked in' : that might be Père Louis
Bouyer, or even Professor Gilson. But Fr. Kelly laid much more
emphasis than they would on an integral connection between the
centralization of Papal government and ideas of divine absolute
sovereignty that began to prevail in the fourteenth century, on the
intimate relation between Calvin's idea of the sovereignty of God
and the history of the Papacy from the Avignon period to the
Renaissance. Some of his connections were much more far-fetched.
He was fond of saying that the Great Wall of China was responsible for the war of 1914. By this he meant that pressure at one end
of the steppes drove the Huns off the other, that they were responsible for the barbarian invasion of the Roman empire, and this for
the antagonism between Germany and France. But quite apart from
the mistake [9] of attributing events in the fourth century to the

[7] Quoted ibid., p. 553 from a letter to Miss Emmet.
[8] The difference would be that Father Kelly would put S. Thomas on one
side of the line, allowing that he was not a Thomist, and Father White on the
other, admitting that he laid himself open to misinterpretation and distortion.
[9] The mistake of course was not entirely his own. Other writers had identified
the Hiung-Nu of Chinese history with the Huns, and even drawn the conclusion that their defeat contributed to the decline and fall of Rome, but the
Han empire in China began to decay at the beginning of the third century,
while the Hun hordes were not seen in the West before the fourth.

achievements of the Han dynasty in the first and second, the antagonism of Roman and Teuton, suggested by Kingsley, is far less important for France and Germany than the difference in their political development between the thirteenth century and the Thirty Years' War. What is important about such statements, right or wrong, is the insistence on the unity of history, on the whole purpose of God controlling the whole, responsible for the discovery of America at the crisis of the Renaissance, for the industrial revolution after the wars of religion. Without such a vision the Christian revelation may come to be regarded as an isolated series of special miracles, and theology as the historical study of responses to these, in the inspired Scriptures, the writings of great theologians, and the definitions of councils and confessions, but dogmatics is more than that.

Dogmatics in this sense is an unfamiliar word to many Anglicans, for the theological schools in the English universities, in marked contrast with those of Scotland and Germany, have for many years devoted most of their attention to the interpretation of Scripture and the history of doctrine, a little to the philosophy and psychology of religion, but very little to the theological interpretation of science, history, and life in general. Fr. Kelly expected little of the theologians, except Temple and Oliver Quick, whom he admired, and with whom he sometimes exchanged letters.[10] But he was much excited by one of the early plays of Dorothy Sayers, and greatly enjoyed an exchange of letters with her, in which both displayed a like pungency in wit. In this epilogue he has been considered almost entirely as a theologian and an interpreter of history, for this was his real office after 1919. The direction of education at Kelham had passed into other hands, though his counsel was often sought, always heard, and frequently followed. He continued to lecture a great deal until about 1934, and a little until 1943, when he was over eighty. Two of his best books, *The Gospel of God* (1928), republished with a memoir in 1959, and *Catholicity* (1932) belong to this last period.

Of his other books, *The History of a Religious Idea* (1898), *Aims and Methods of Theological Study*, *The Continuation of*

[10] I have quoted from one of these in the memoir attached to *The Gospel of God*, p. 32.

Study, and *An Idea in the Working* (1908), are concerned with the aims and objects of the S.S.M. *England and the Church* (1902) and *The Church and Religious Unity* (1913) are of great historical interest for those concerned with the situation at the beginning of the century, and with the early history of the ecumenical movement, but they hardly speak to the present day. *The History of the Church of Christ,* in two volumes (1901–2), covers only the first five centuries, and was perhaps premature. It is less revealing than his later lectures, whose bulk precludes their publication entire. Of pamphlets, published articles, and unpublished lectures and papers, the sheer quantity makes selection very difficult.

The main framework of this book is provided by an autobiography written in about 1929–31, but ending in 1919. This has been supplemented and in places replaced from

1. Personal Thoughts Concerning Unity, a memorandum which amounts to a history of Fr. Kelly's theological outlook, dated 1927.
2. *The History of a Religious Idea,* published in 1898, long out of print and now rare.
3. *Ad filios,* written for the students at Kelham in 1920–1.
4. An article, 'Diamond Jubilee of the Mousehole,' published in the *S.S.M. Quarterly Paper,* Vol. 51, No. 177, in December 1950, just after his death, and written shortly before it.
5. *An Idea in the Working,* published in 1908, and republished in 1927 and 1953. This I have used more sparingly, since it is still in print. The references are to the present edition.

I have also used

1. The addresses given in the Holy Week Retreat in 1893, just before the Society of the Sacred Mission was formally inaugurated.
2. Some extracts from *Ad fratres,* written for the brethren in 1906.
3. Part of Fr. Kelly's statement to the General Chapter at the time of his resignation as Director in May 1910.
4. Some other extracts from an article and a letter relating to the World Missionary Conference at Edinburgh in 1910, with his speech from the *Report.*

5. A memorandum presented to John R. Mott at the time of his visit to America in 1912, with a comment from Neville Talbot.
6. Extracts from letters about Japan to the Revd. Lawrence Rose, now Dean of the General Theological Seminary, New York.

I am indebted to the last-named for permission to print the last item.

Throughout I have tried to omit what is redundant, or too allusive to be understood, and occasionally corrected what is grammatically obscure. My own editorial contribution consists of notes. Of these the most important are

1. On his family background. In this I have drawn extensively from an account of his father written by his brother, Fr. Alfred Kelly, and annotated by himself.
2. On theological education in the Church of England in 1890, and on some of the problems raised by the limitations and defects of this.
3. On the relationship in the order of time between the Community of the Resurrection and the Society of the Sacred Mission.
4. On changes in the conditions of admission to the College of the S.S.M. in and after 1902.
5. On the circumstances of Father Kelly's resignation as Director in 1910.
6. On the beginnings of the ecumenical movement.
7. On Fr. Kelly's life and thought after 1919, by way of an epilogue.
8. Some important dates.

G.E.

HERBERT HAMILTON KELLY, 1860–1950

1860 July 18th. Born in Manchester.

1872–7 Manchester Grammar School.

1878–9 Royal Military Academy, Woolwich.

1879–83 Queen's College, Oxford. B.A., fourth class honours in history, 1883.

1883–5 Ordained deacon and priest to Leeds, near Maidstone, Kent.

1886 Toynbee Hall : Holy Trinity, Dalston (April–June).

1886–90 In charge of S. Barnabas', Southfields, in the parish of S. Paul, Wimbledon.

1890 December 31st. The Korean Missionary Brotherhood at 97 Vassall Road, Kennington, South London.

1892 September 29th : this name changed to the Society of the Sacred Mission.

1893 May 9th. Fr. Kelly began his novitiate. He was professed September 29th, 1894.

1897 February 18th–20th. The Society moved to Mildenhall.

1901 Visit to South Africa and beginnings there.

1903 July 29th–August 5th. The move from Mildenhall to Kelham.

1907–8 First contacts with the Student Christian Movement.

1910 May 31st. Fr. Kelly ceased to be Director.

1912 His visit to America.

1913–15 and 1916–19 His work in Japan.

1919 He returned to Kelham, and lectured until 1943.

1950 October 31st. He died.

INDEX

Ad filios, 45–6, 47, 54–5, 86–8, 88–90, 137
Ad fratres, 91–5, 134, 137
Africa, 10–11, 46, 60, 68, 81–2, 87, 89, 98–9
America, 118–28, 136, 138–9
Asceticism, 16–17, 52, 65–8, 72, 94–5
Ashton-under-Lyne, 20, 25, 29–30
Athanasian creed, 48
Augustine, S., 51–2, 92
Autobiography (*c.* 1930), 21–40, 53–4, 79–80, 83–4, 99–101, 106, 124–7, 137

Baillie, John, 134
Barth, Karl, 10, 13–14, 133–4
Benedictines, 61–2, 71–2
Biblical criticism, 13–15
Biblical theology, 14, 16, 33, 51, 54, 94, 127
Biology, 13, 16
Bonhoeffer, Dietrich, 13
Broad Church, 32, 91–2
Brooke, Canon C., 44–6
Bull, Paul, C. R., 96

Calvin, 51, 135
Cambridge, 41, 53, 85
Chemistry, 23–4
China, 11, 63, 69, 129, 135–6
Christian Brothers, 72
Church and Religious Unity, The, 118, 137
C.M.S., 76, 126, 128
Constitution of S.S.M., 72–6, 79–82, 102, 106

Conversion, 26, 28–9, 132
Corfe, Bishop Charles, 44–5
Couturier, Paul, 5, 8
Cowley Fathers, 94, 103, 125
Cricket, 22, 28–9, 36, 39–40
Cunningham, Canon B. K., 14–15

Dalston, Holy Trinity, 38, 47
Darwin and Darwinism, 13, 42
Davidson, Randall, Bishop and Archbishop, 7, 82, plate 6
Deafness, 28, 131
Dogmatics, 13–17, 48–53, 55, 91–3, 101, 127–8, 132–6
Dominicans, 63, 79
Drake, H., S.S.M., 85, 98

Ecumenical movement, 5–8, 48, 107–24, 133–4, 138
Edinburgh Conference, 1910, 5–6, 107–8, 110–18, 137
Eliot, T. S., 133
Emmet, D. M., 134–5

Farrar, Archdeacon F. W., 32, 65
Football, 29, 49, 55, 84–5, 90
Franciscans and Friars in general, 61–2, 68

Gore, Charles, afterwards Bishop, 7, 84, 96, 100, 108, 132
Greek, 28, 35

Hebert, A. G., S.S.M., 15n., 134
Hegel and Hegelianism, 53, 126–7, 129, 131–2
Hermits, 60–1, 63

INDEX

History, 13, 16, 34–5, 47, 58–64, 70–2, 131, 135–6
History of a Religious Idea (1898), 82–3, 136–7
Holland, Canon H. S., 39, 44
Holy Week addresses, 1893, 56–79, 81, 137
Hooft, W. H. Visser 't, 10, 134

Idea in the Working (1908), 46, 55–6, 81–2, 84–6, 88, 137
India, 11, 63, 125

James, William, 53, 120
Japan, 5, 10–12, 63, 106, 125–30, 138
Jenks, D., S.S.M., 98–9
Jesuits, 62–3, 68–9, 79, 84

Kelly, A. D., S.S.M., 19–21, 98, 131, 138
Kelly, Edith Mary (sister of Fr. Kelly), 21, 26
Kelly, Francis (brother), 21, 25–6
Kelly, Canon J. D. (father), 19–20, 25–7, 36
Kelly, Margaret (mother), 19–21, 25, 110–11
Kennington, 5, 37, 44–7, 55–6, 81–4, 96, 98, plates 2–4
Kingsley, Charles, 28–32, 35, 132, 136
Korea, 44–5, 81–2, 85, 87, 98

Latin, 23, 54
Lay-brothers, 43, 86–7
Luther, 33

Manchester, 19–21, 25–6, 36, 139
Mason, Canon A. J., 37
Mathematics, 22–4, 28, 30, 34

Maurice, F. D., 10, 15, 30–5, 38, 51–2, 127, 132, 133n.
Mildenhall, 5, 83, 85–8, 96, 98, plates 3–4
Mirfield, 84, 88, 96, 99, 103, 138
Modernism, 9–11, 32, 91–2, 118–23, 129, 133
Mott, J. R., 107, 111, 118n., 123–4, 138

Newman, Cardinal, 45, 93–4, 133

Orthodox Church, 7, 10, 107, 123n., 124n.
Oxford, 19, 24, 28–37, 41, 50, 93

Paton, the Revd. D. M., 5–16
Paton, the Revd. W., 8
Personal Thoughts Concerning Unity (1927), 47–53, 108–10, 118
Philosophy, 13, 16, 30, 34–7, 50, 53–4, 70, 92, 107, 126, 131–2
Physics, 16, 23
Plato, 35–6
Predestination, 51–3, 55
Psychology, 13, 25, 31, 53, 120, 126, 128
Pusey, Dr. E. B., 48

Quarterly Paper of S.S.M., 44–5, 112–18, 137
Quick, Canon O. C., 136

Reformation, 57, 62, 131, 133, 135
Rock-climbing, 39, 130
Roman Catholicism, 6, 8, 10, 32, 48, 62–3, 65, 68, 107, 123–4, 132, 134–5

141

Rose, the Revd. L., 128–30, 138
Rowing, 29

Sayers, Miss D. L., 136
Science, 13, 16, 20n., 22, 29–30, 37, 129, 131
S.C.M., 6–9, 17, 104, 107–10, 118, 120, 133
Southfields, 38–40, 47, 79, plate 2
S.P.C.K. College in Stepney, 43
S.P.G., 7, 77, 112, 126, 128

Talbot, Bishop E. S., 7, 82, 85, 108

Talbot, Neville, afterwards Bishop, 6–7, 53, 100–1, 108, 118, 123–4, 138
Temple, William, Bishop and Archbishop, 9, 39, 108, 134–6
Thomas Aquinas, S., 23, 51, 53, 64, 68, 70, 133, 135

Wesley, John, 92, 131–3
Woodward, H.W., S.S.M., 81–2, plate 3
Woolwich, 23, 26–8, 139

Y.M.C.A., 119–24

Zen Buddhism, 11, 130

CONTENTS

WITH SOURCES

editorial comments indicated by italic type

INTRODUCTION   *page* 5

by the Reverend D. M. Paton

1. CHILDHOOD AND YOUTH   19
      from *Autobiography*
   The Family Background
      from notes compiled by Fr. Kelly and his brother

2. OXFORD   28
      from *Autobiography*

3. ORDINATION   36
      from *Autobiography*

4. *Note*   41
   THEOLOGICAL EDUCATION
      from S.S.M. Quarterly Paper, Vol. 51, No. 177, Decem-
      ber 1950; *Ad filios; An Idea in the Working; Personal
      Thoughts Concerning Unity; Autobiography*

5. ADDRESSES ON THE RELIGIOUS LIFE   57
      Holy Week, 1893; also from *Autobiography*

6. FROM KENNINGTON TO KELHAM   81
      from *An Idea in the Working; History of a Religious
      Idea; Autobiography; Ad filios; Ad fratres*
   Kelham and Mirfield
   The College after 1902

7. *Note*   98
   RESIGNATION IN 1910
      from *Autobiography; Statement, May 31st, 1910*
   Note

8. *Note*   107

   ŒCUMENICA

   from *Personal Thoughts Concerning Unity;* letter to his
   mother, June 29th, 1910; *World Missionary Conference,*
   1910, supplement to the *Report of Commission,* V, p. 312;
   S.S.M. Quarterly Paper, September 1910 (Vol. IX,
   No. 35); *The Present Condition of Theological Movement in America*

9. JAPAN   125

   from *Autobiography;* letter to the Revd. L. Rose
   Note

EPILEGOMENA

EDITORIAL EPILOGUE   131

SOME IMPORTANT DATES   139

INDEX   140